GIRLS WHO BUILD

DISCLAIMER: Working with tools inherently includes the risk of injury, and projects undertaken based on the information in this book is at your own risk. The author and publisher disclaim any liabilities for any injuries or property damage caused in any way by the content of this book.

Black Dog & Leventhal Publishers
Hachette Book Group
1290 Avenue of the Americas
New York, NY 10104

www.hachettebookgroup.com
www.blackdogandleventhal.com

First Edition: October 2020

Black Dog & Leventhal Publishers is an imprint of Perseus Books, LLC, a subsidiary of Hachette Book Group, Inc. The Black Dog & Leventhal Publishers name and logo are trademarks of Hachette Book Group, Inc.

The publisher is not responsible for websites (or their content) that are not owned by the publisher.

The Hachette Speakers Bureau provides a wide range of authors for speaking events. To find out more, go to www.HachetteSpeakersBureau.com or call (866) 376-6591.

Additional credits information is on page 255.

Print book interior design by Frances J. Soo Ping Chow.

LCCN: 2020930992

ISBNs: 978-0-7624-6721-1 (hardcover),
978-0-7624-6720-4 (paperback),
978-0-7624-6722-8 (ebook)

Printed in China

1010

10 9 8 7 6 5 4 3 2 1

GIRLS WHO BUILD

INSPIRING **CURIOSITY** AND **CONFIDENCE** TO **MAKE ANYTHING POSSIBLE**

KATIE HUGHES
founder of Girls Build

Illustrated by Kay Coenen

BLACK DOG
& LEVENTHAL
PUBLISHERS
NEW YORK

CONTENTS

INTRODUCTION

I took my first carpentry job when I was twenty-two years old and fresh out of college (or, in my case, fresh off my postcollege AmeriCorps year with Habitat for Humanity) so I could pay rent and eat food. I saw carpentry as a gig, not a career. My career, I thought, would involve sheltering the shelterless, feeding the foodless, or doing anything befitting a humanitarian poster—the kind of work my social work degree had promised. But in the meantime, I was happy to swing a hammer, fine-tune my woodworking skills, and learn from a man who quickly became my mentor and friend.

I'd built a good base of house-framing knowledge from my AmeriCorps supervisor, Ray, who teased us by saying, "Some bosses are tough and ruthless; I'm just rough and toothless." Calling Ray rough is a stretch. He was funny and kind, believed that the three women on his crew were equal to the men, and took it in stride when we pointed out the ways we weren't treated as such. I fell in love with building that year and started on an unexpected career, one that was actually rooted in my childhood. In a way, Girls Build—the nonprofit I eventually founded to teach girls to gain skills and confidence in the trades—grew out of that foundation too.

The first time I used a tool, I was about two or three. My dad, Jim, had died tragically and suddenly at the age of thirty-seven after an on-the-job fall from a telephone pole. At the time, I was just a tiny heartbeat in my mom's womb; she intended to surprise my dad by announcing her pregnancy to him on a Christmas card. He had no idea my mom was pregnant.

What we had left of him was a garage full of tools that he had loved and had used to build our house and fix our many broken cars and make a cradle, a dollhouse, a rocking horse, and whatever else struck my two older sisters' whims. Those tools were symbols of his love and affection for my sisters—and for me, too, I always believed. He'd held them in his hands for hours and hours. Our hands could touch those same spots, hold his tools in the same way, and we could feel a little of what he might have felt as he built for us. It seemed, just a tiny bit, like he was there with us.

The first project I remember tackling was our

front-yard tree fort, complete with a swing and a cat elevator. I was three years old. Bridget, four years my senior, was the project manager. She guided my pudgy hands onto the drill, helping me bore holes into a 2x6 for our swing. Then, later, she handed me Daddy's hammer, our most precious of all his tools, along with a scoop of nails. I nailed up some of the steps that led us precariously into the upper reaches of the tree.

Of the whole fort, though, the cat elevator was the most important piece, precisely because it was the most ridiculous. First, to get this point out of the way, yes, cats have built-in elevators commonly called "claws" that they use daily to climb trees. Apparently, according to us, our cat, Bubbles, needed something fancier—something in the form of two thin ropes thrown over a tree limb with loops at the bottom. We would slide poor Bubbles into said loops, then haul her up into the fort. She hated it, but we thought we were ingenious.

The imagination involved in creating that cat elevator is what I attempt to encourage at our Girls Build summer camps. I want girls to leave feeling like they could build something as absurd and unnecessary as a cat elevator. I want them to draw it out on paper, on a whiteboard at school, or on the sidewalk in chalk. I want them to make Popsicle-stick models of it, fold an origami version of it, or do whatever else they feel like doing. I want them to be excited and inspired by a product of their own creativity. I want them to go home and build a freaking cat elevator.

When I started Girls Build in 2016, I had run a similar program for eight years under the umbrella of another nonprofit organization. Shortly after I left, they cut the program. I didn't realize how important the education offered by that program had been to local tradeswomen until they began inundating me with requests to continue it. I'd like to say that I took their subtle hints, but really it wasn't until one of them essentially smacked me over the head with the idea of starting a nonprofit of my own that I realized that, a decade and a half out of college, I was uniquely positioned to run a nonprofit that teaches girls to build. This surprised me. When I look over my shoulder at the past fifteen years I think, "Huh. I never realized it was all leading here."

In our first year, we held two weeks of camp at the University of Portland (in Oregon) and served eighty girls. In 2019, we held eleven weeks of camp in five locations and served nearly four hundred girls over one summer alone. We've grown.

Over the course of any given day at camp, girls attend four workshops and use as many tools as we can put in their hands. LeShayla, a camper from our first year, lived with her grandma and had a fantastic experience at camp. She was nine during her first time at camp, loved woodworking and building a playhouse, and really fell in love with the tools. One tool specifically.

"So, apparently I need to buy LeShayla an . . . impact driver?" her grandma asked with hesitation, leaning on her walker on the last day of camp. I laughed, picturing LeShayla chatting

construction with her grandma over dinner. And she wasn't the last grandma to come to me with tool questions. Not two weeks ago, I got an email requesting a list. "My granddaughters attended your camp last summer, and for Christmas they want 'all the tools from Girls Build.' Can you send me a list?"

It is the ease with which girls learn the lingo and the tools that sticks with me. The first day of camp is quiet. The girls seem weighed down by all the tools and safety equipment. Then, truly overnight, they turn into these confident little beings who don't need help clasping their tool belts or remembering which tool is the speed square. They find they are capable of installing a solar panel (and using the energy to toast a Pop-Tart), soldering copper, pouring concrete, and stopping a 20′ water-main leak. They also realize that they might drive a nail into the wrong spot, cut a board too short, paint something the wrong color, or make twenty other mistakes in a single day—and that the day is not ruined, projects are not broken, life is not over. Essentially, failure is not the end, and soon they brush off mistakes quickly, give each other tips on repairing damage, and keep moving forward.

On the last day of camp, when the girls are wild, loud, and somewhat preposterous as they tour their parents and guardians around, I make sure to position myself near what is commonly called the chop saw, a stationary tool that sits on its own stand and features a 12″ blade. Formally, it's known as a sliding compound miter saw. To operate it, girls must reach up to the handle, hit the trigger, and lower the blade through a piece of wood. To parental eyes, it can look terrifying. It's time to show off, though, and each girl walks up confidently.

She does all the prerequisite measuring and safety steps, and finally rests her fingers on the trigger, ready to cut. It's at that moment that her parents, who have clearly been holding back, look to her and say, "Are you sure you can use this?" It's like they waited until the last second, knowing they sent her to camp for this very tool, for this very lesson, and for her to use it with confidence. They can't help themselves—they even hate themselves for it—but the words escape their mouths almost involuntarily.

Then comes the response.

No matter if she is ten or fourteen, she simultaneously huffs and slowly, meticulously, delivers the best eye roll imaginable.

"Of course I can use a chop saw," she mutters, as if a chop saw were a pencil or tricycle or one of those little cars kids push with their feet. Of course she can. Duh.

She then hits the trigger, her shoulders thrown back in slight defiance, her cut as perfect as if I'd cut it. Then she blows off the sawdust with a little extra swagger.

I love that swagger. And I've started to think of the eye roll as the Girls Build litmus test.

Did she roll her eyes at her parents for doubting her ability to handle the 12″ sliding compound miter saw? Yes?

Mission accomplished.

HOW TO USE THIS BOOK

There are a few things you should know about this book. First, the girls in this book are so rad that I wanted to be friends with all of them. Next, we put some thought into how we organized the book to make it easy to use. Let's dig in.

The book has the following sections:

SAFETY GEAR

Safety always comes first. Make sure you read this section before starting any skills or projects.

TERMINOLOGY

This is where I tell you more about the words and phrases I'll be using throughout the book, and the best way to interpret them.

TOOLS

This list includes all the tools the girls used to complete their projects, and the ones you'll need if you want to build the projects yourselves. Please don't go buy tools right away. See what you can borrow from friends and neighbors. Not only is that free, but it's more fun. And while you are at it, see if they have cut off any of their fingers. If not, get a lesson on that tool from them.

SKILLS

In this section, I go over, in a very basic way, how to hammer, drill, saw, and perform many other skills.

THE GIRLS

Take a gander at the photos, then read the interviews. These girls are so interesting. I may have cried at a few of the interviews because I found these kids so inspiring and insightful. Take time to get into their stories. You won't regret it.

THE PROJECTS

The book starts with the easier projects and then moves on to the harder ones. I suggest that you, too, begin with an early project and work your way through the book. As you do each project, you will learn something new that will help you with the next one.

 This illustration tells you how closely someone needs to be watching you, and how much help you might need. One pair of safety glasses means someone should watch you, but you can do it all yourself. Four pairs means that you will need an adult to do some parts for you. If you are an adult, one pair of safety glasses means you can do it on your own. Four means you need some classes under your belt, or a skilled friend at your side.

 This illustration is pretty self-explanatory. One dollar sign is pretty dang cheap. Four is expensive. Nothing in this book cost us more than $100, excluding tool purchases. Again, beg or borrow tools before you run out and buy them.

 This illustration shows you what level of skill is needed to do a project. The first project is rated as one hammer—no skills necessary. The last is rated four hammers, and you will have to work yourself up to it.

 This illustration tells you the amount of time a project will take. Four clocks is up to a whole day, depending upon skill level. Two clocks is half a day. You get the idea.

WORK SURFACE: This tells you on what surface you need to complete the project safely. Most of the time you will need a sturdy, flat surface that is clampable, like a table, but sometimes you may only need a wide-open area.

MATERIALS: These are items you will use up while making the project, like wood or screws.

TOOLS: These are the tools you will need for the project. When possible I list more than one option, like a jigsaw or chop saw.

STEPS: I have tested the steps described for each project, and we hope that between the descriptions, the drawings, and the illustrations you will have plenty of information to complete each one.

ADULT SUPERVISION

Should you have an adult with you at all times while you build? Yes. Even for projects rated one pair of safety glasses, you will always need an adult by your side. If nothing else, it's never good to work alone. A buddy of any age can help you apply a Band-Aid if you are cut, and a smart buddy will remind you to put on safety glasses when you forget. My firm recommendation is to have your buddy be one of your favorite adults who will help hold the drill when you need an extra boost, or use that chop saw when you can't.

MATERIALS GLOSSARY

At the end of the book appears a list of many of the materials used in the projects, as well as a few other basic building materials you should know about. My hope is not only that you will reference the list as you work through each project, but that you might read through it ahead of time. I find all this construction talk fascinating, and I hope you do too. You may not. Not yet, at least. But maybe someday you will geek out about it as much as I do.

OTHER THINGS

I have written a book that I would want to read: one that is full of stories, personal anecdotes, and the real scoop on tools and materials. I want you to know the tools that are bunk and the skills that are really rad. I want you to know the reality you will face when you walk into a hardware store, and I want you to walk in with as much secret knowledge as I can pack into these pages.

SAFETY GEAR

I run a nonprofit that teaches building to children. It is my number-one priority that everyone have a great time and stay safe while we're together. My goal is the same for this book. Aside from reading the directions clearly, seeking outside help, and researching techniques and tools, an important part of staying safe is using the proper safety gear. The items listed below are all things that I wear at home while working casually on a project, or at my job when I'm working on something serious. The way I think about it, you will never regret being extra safe.

SAFETY GLASSES

Once you find a style of glasses you like, buy two pairs of them. You may eventually lose them, or they will get scratched, and you don't want to get stuck in the middle of your project without safety glasses. I keep safety glasses in my car, in my house, in my workshop, in my basement. It never hurts to have a pair within reach wherever you are working.

These are the glasses I like (see illustration), but you might find something else that fits your face better. What you are looking for is safety glasses that hug your eye sockets, allowing little room for debris to get in from above, below, or the sides. I once got a shard of metal in my eye that came *around* my safety glasses, because I borrowed a friend's that didn't fit me well.

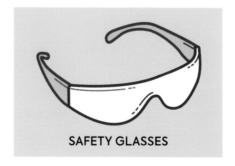

SAFETY GLASSES

I use glasses like these because they come in a few different sizes, they are comfortable, they are very easy to find, and, honestly, they're pretty cheap.

You already wear glasses, you say? You still need to wear safety glasses over your glasses. This kind can be large and bulky and aren't my favorite, but your eyes are worth it. Option B? Find out if your glasses are shatterproof. If they are, you can get pieces of plastic that attach to the ear pieces of your glasses and protect your eyes from projectiles coming at you from the left or right. In my opinion these aren't as great as the ones that go over your glasses. Option C, for once you really nerd out? Get prescription safety glasses.

EAR PROTECTION

Ear damage is permanent. Once I realized this, I finally put on the earmuffs that my friend Dawn gave me for my birthday, because she cares about me more than I do. It's important to protect your ears so you don't end up being that person who just smiles and laughs when people talk to you because you have no idea what they said. It's awkward. Trust me.

You have two routes to go with ear protection. The simplest option is to get protective earmuffs. You can use them in most scenarios, and they are large enough that you probably won't lose them. You want to protect your ears at roughly the 100-decibel level (I am telling you this so you will bring this knowledge with you as you shop). This will cover the noise put out by table saws, chop saws, drills, and any other power tool in this book.

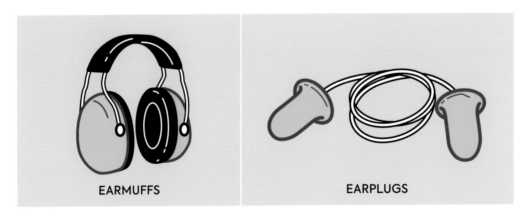

EARMUFFS   EARPLUGS

It doesn't hurt to buy a few disposable earplugs to keep handy, just in case you can't find your earmuffs. I like the kind on a string with a very squishy foam. Some are cone shaped—I hate those—and some have the string sticking all the way through the foam. You can't feel it, but in your heart you know it's close to poking your eardrum. Go to the hardware store and start smushing earplugs until you find one that you like. To properly put it in, roll it between your fingers so the narrow end comes to a point. Insert the now pointy, narrow end into your ear (not too hard), and hold the exterior end in place for a few seconds. You will hear the foam filling up your ear canal and cutting off sound. Do this in both ears, and be on your way.

ATTIRE

Wear closed-toe shoes when you are working to give your toes some protection. Wear long sleeves when possible. On hot days, wear a T-shirt instead of a tank top—you want to protect your skin as much as you can—and long pants, preferably jeans with no holes, instead of something like leggings. There is obviously flexibility here—I love working in shorts and a tank top on hot days—but the more skin you expose, the more cuts and scrapes you can get on that skin.

Make sure your clothes fit well. Don't wear loose or oversized clothes—trade out that big, baggy, comfy hoodie for one that is fairly tight on your body. Pull your hair into a ponytail if it's long. If you lean over and your hair hangs down into your work, put it up in a bun. Don't wear jewelry on your hands, wrists, or neck—even rings can be a hazard. Essentially, you want to minimize anything that can get caught in a tool or machine. Tuck the strings of your hoodie inside your sweatshirt, or get rid of the strings entirely. If you wear a head scarf, make sure it is tied back. As you start work, do a quick evaluation of what you are wearing and make sure it's safe.

HARD HAT

I would be remiss if I didn't mention hard hats. Most people working in shops don't wear hard hats. But if you are working with a lot of people, moving a lot of large objects, or have anyone working above you, put a hard hat on. You won't regret it.

HARD HAT

TERMINOLOGY

CROW'S FOOT: This is a V-shaped mark that precisely indicates a measurement. Instead of a dot or straight line, the crow's foot is clear, easy to find later, and, most importantly, precise. See page 30 to learn how to draw a crow's foot.

DOMINANT HAND: What hand do you write with? That is your dominant hand.

FLUSH: This is when two boards share a joint without one being positioned farther out than the other. The two boards are set even with each other with no overhang.

NARROW END OF BOARD: Unless your board is a square, one side will be longer than the other, like a rectangle. The narrow end is the shorter side.

OVERHANG: When two pieces of material (wood, mostly, but sometimes metal) are placed together, sometimes one piece hangs over the edge of the other. Sometimes you want this, sometimes you don't.

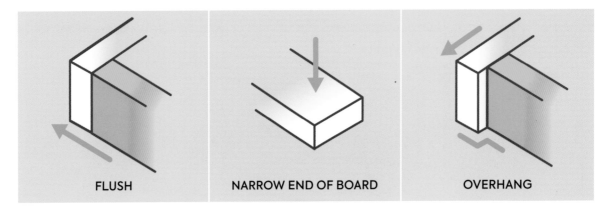

FLUSH   NARROW END OF BOARD   OVERHANG

PENCILS, CARPENTRY PENCILS, AND MARKERS: Normal pencils are round, and you can use them for most of the projects in this book. Carpentry pencils are flat with a rectangular body so they won't roll away when you set them on a table or sloped surface. A permanent marker is good to use for marking sheet metal or other metal, like copper. A fine-tipped permanent marker is best.

PILOT HOLE: This is the hole you drill to make a path for a screw to go nicely into a piece of wood. It's not always necessary to drill a pilot hole before driving a screw, but sometimes it's the best option. If you are just learning how to use a drill, a pilot hole will help the screw go in easy peasy.

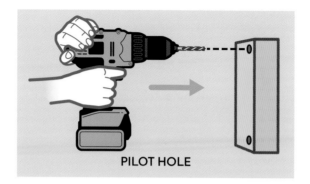

PILOT HOLE

SNUGGED UP: This is when your pieces of wood are pushed together as tightly as they can be, which is a good goal to aim for. Please note, this is not a technical term, but I use it a lot anyway.

TOENAILING: This means to connect two pieces of material with a screw or nail going in at an angle from one piece into the other. See page 39 to learn how to toenail.

WASTE SIDE OF THE LINE: When you have measured a board and drawn a line through that measurement, one side of the line is the piece you are keeping, and the other is the waste side. Write your measurement on the good side, or the side you are keeping. That way, you'll know which side to keep, and it also helps you remember the length of the board for later in the project.

TOOLS

Tools are expensive. Some are more expensive than others. Adults, if you buy a low-quality impact driver for $50, you will buy that same impact driver over and over as it breaks after an average amount of use. Or you can buy one drill and driver set for $150 to $300, and never buy another drill or driver again. This is the better choice all around, so save yourself some dollars, get excited, and go buy that nice drill and driver set you've been eyeing for months. The same goes for hand tools, but the price difference is much smaller. A plastic speed square is about $3, and a thick, metal, top-of-the-line speed square is $10. Get the $10 one. It comes with a book, so you can geek out learning all kinds of things you never knew, and you'll have that speed square your whole life.

Here is a list of the tools you will need to do the projects in this book. Don't run out and buy all of them, unless that's something you like to do. Most of the projects are simple and only require a few items. You can always borrow from neighbors or friends, or see if your town has a tool library.

CLAMPS

Pipe clamps and bar clamps are essentially the same, but pipe clamps tend to be longer and are used in professional wood shops. Bar clamps are smaller and are perfectly great for any project you are working on from this book.

C-clamps are less commonly used in woodworking, but if you have some at home, they may work for holding down a piece of wood on a table. They will not work for many of the projects in this book, though. My suggestion is to invest in two 36" bar clamps.

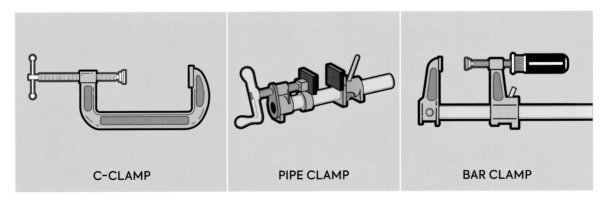

C-CLAMP   PIPE CLAMP   BAR CLAMP

CROWBAR

A crowbar is primarily used to pull wood apart. It looks like a large, metal candy cane with a slightly curved stem. It has a claw on the end, like a hammer does, which will pull nails out easily when you have to take apart a project.

DRILL AND IMPACT DRIVER

A drill is a handheld power tool that bores holes.

An impact driver looks like a drill but has a shorter nose. The impact driver is a great tool that hammers as it turns, making driving a screw much easier, especially for kids. It reduces the possibility that you will strip a screw (hollowing out the head of the screw so you can no longer drive it), as long as you use it correctly.

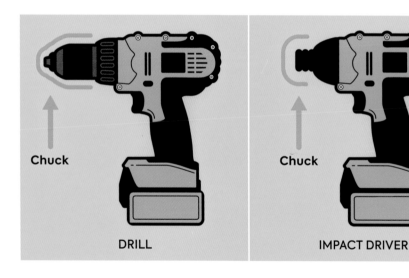

Chuck

The chuck is the part of the drill that opens and closes around a bit. By spinning the outer ring, three prongs inside come together to clutch the bit tightly.

DRILL BITS

The term "drill bit" is used by most people to refer to two different items: a bit that bores holes, and a bit that drives screws. A rare handful of people call the bits that bore holes "twist bits," but no one I've ever worked with has. It is a nice differentiating name, but people don't commonly say it, so that means you're left with possible confusion about which type of bit is being referred to. The good news is that in this book, I've included enough information to tell you which bit you need. For example, if the instructions ask for a ⅛" drill bit, that would be a bit that bores a hole. But if the instructions tell you to use a #3 Phillips, you are looking for a bit that drives a screw. If there is a fraction in front of the term "drill bit" or "bit," you are looking for a long, thin piece of metal that will make a hole for you. Otherwise, you are looking for something that will drive a screw. See, not so bad.

Bits to Bore Holes, or Twist Bits

Bits used to bore holes come in many different sizes and materials, the most common being bits for boring into wood, or wood bits. It's actually incredible to walk through the drill bit aisle at your local hardware store to see the wide variety that are available. You can get bits that will drill through thick metal as easily as they bore through wood. Pretty cool.

Drill bits are called out by the size of the hole they bore. A ⅛" drill bit is ⅛" in diameter and will bore a hole that size. A ⅝" bit will bore a ⅝" hole, and so on. Not too complicated. You can buy them individually, but for now it's probably best to simply buy a set that contains a variety of sizes. For this book you will need the ⅛", ⁵⁄₁₆", ⅜", and ⅝" bits.

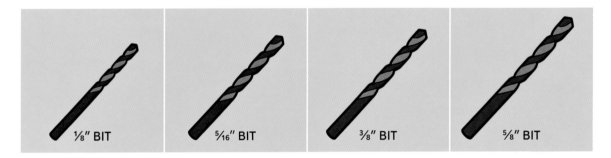

⅛" BIT   ⁵⁄₁₆" BIT   ⅜" BIT   ⅝" BIT

Countersinking Bit

A countersinking bit makes a hole that lets a screw sit below the surface of the wood.

Forstner Bit

A Forstner bit is really great. It is a wide circular bit that drills a nice, clean hole. Driving it can require more force and strength than driving a regular bit or a spade bit, but for making larger holes ¾" or larger, I think it is a little easier to use because of its shape.

Spade Bit

A spade bit is a flat bit that bores a big hole. Soleil used one on her magnet board (see Project 10: Soleil's Magnet Board). Spade bits are fine, but if given the choice, most builders will choose the (more expensive) Forstner bit for larger holes, or even a large twist bit.

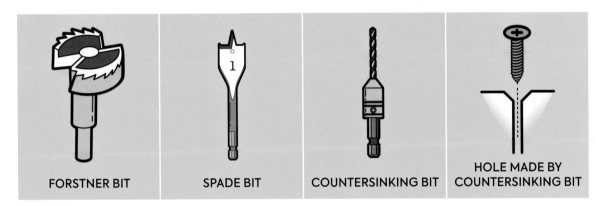

| FORSTNER BIT | SPADE BIT | COUNTERSINKING BIT | HOLE MADE BY COUNTERSINKING BIT |

Bits to Drive Screws

There are many different types of bits to drive screws, and it's important to understand the differences between them. If you try to use the wrong bit for a screw, you may end up stripping the screw and causing myriad problems, or simply being unable to complete your project. Tip: The majority of boxes of screws come with the right drill bit (or bit tip) inside. Take a look at the box for wording that says something like "bit inside." Also, more great news: Most drill bits have the size engraved on them. For a Phillips #3, it will say "PH3." For a Torx #25 star bit, it will say "T25." You're welcome.

Flathead or Slotted Bit

Flathead or slotted screws are no longer very common, but it's important to know about them. They can be found in older buildings and furniture. They are difficult to work with and strip easily. The key in removing them is to keep applying pressure on the screw and back out very slowly. You can still buy these at the store—but unless it's your only option, don't. One place you will see them is on the plates that go around electrical outlets and light switches. They come in three sizes—1, 2, and 3. The screws that are used in outlets and switchplates are #1, the smallest. The biggest size is #3. Not exactly a complicated system.

Phillips Bit

A Phillips-head screw has a top (or head) that looks like a plus sign. Phillips-head screws are easier to drive and remove than flathead/slotted screws. There are a few variations on the Phillips bit:

- Phillips #1: This screw has a very small and thin "plus sign" and is used for small items. Most likely you will use a screwdriver for these screws, not a drill or impact driver.

- Phillips #2: This is the most common Phillips bit, and the most common screw. It's usually an indicator of a very basic screw that someone hasn't put a ton of thought into. These screws also strip easily. One exception? Drywall screws. These screws are usually Phillips #2, and they work well for that application.

- Phillips #3: This screw head is wider and has a plus sign that is blunted at the bottom and has a square hollow at the center. If you use a #2 bit on a #3 screw, you will strip your screw. Tip: You can also use a square bit in the #3 Phillips.

Square Bit

The head of a square screw, as the name implies, has a square hole. The screw bits come in various sizes, commonly called #1, #2, #3. For the most part, you will be working with a #2 square bit, but on rare occasions, for something like a trim-head screw, you might need a #1. Again, check the box of screws, and make sure you have a bit to match.

Star or Torx Bit

Star drive screws (that's what everyone calls them, but Torx is their technical name) are great, and a preference for many builders. They allow for a great grip on the screw by the bit. There are different sizes of star bits, and they all start with a T (I'm guessing that stands for Torx). The most common star bits are T15, T20, and T25. One isn't better than another; it's just a matter of which screw you are using. Make sure you check, and get the corresponding bit. (I just found out that these screws are also called hexalobular internals. Go throw that around at the hardware store—and everyone will stare at you with no idea what you are talking about.)

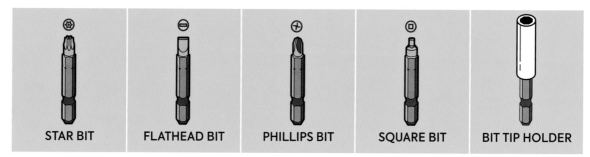

| STAR BIT | FLATHEAD BIT | PHILLIPS BIT | SQUARE BIT | BIT TIP HOLDER |

Drill Bit Sets

If you are ready to invest in your drilling skills, start with a drill bit set that includes most of what you need. Commonly, you will need to buy two sets—one to bore holes and one to drive screws—but you can find some mega sets out there that include both. Note that these kits include the bit tips and the bit tip holder. While you are at the hardware store, invest in a few more bit tip holders, because you will be lost without one.

Bit Tips

A bit tip is a very short version of a regular bit, includes the end that drives the screw, and is intended to go into a bit tip holder (I will get into that). It's like a little baby that needs to be carried, and the thing to carry it is the bit tip holder. Using this system allows for quick changes of just the bit tips, instead of having to open the chuck on the drill each time you want to change bit types. This is a very common system to use, but you can buy longer bits that can be secured into the drill by opening and closing the chuck.

A bit tip holder is shaped like a round metal pencil where someone has drilled a hole into the end and then stuck a magnet in the hole. When you slide a drill bit into the hole, the magnet holds the bit in place. You can now drive a screw. See illustration.

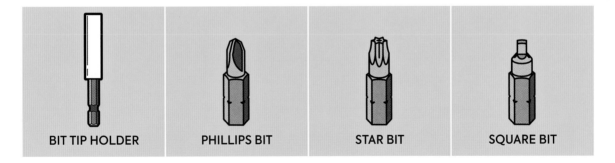

BIT TIP HOLDER   PHILLIPS BIT   STAR BIT   SQUARE BIT

HAMMER

Hammers come in all shapes and sizes. Chances are that the hammer you have lying around your house is a finish hammer: It has a small, smooth head, a shorter handle, a curved claw. Was I right? That type of hammer is perfectly great for any of the projects in this book, I promise. By the end of the book you are going to want to run out and buy a fancy hammer, which is *completely understandable*. Don't let anyone tell you otherwise. Just do some research and buy one you will love.

How to Make Sure It All Works: Thoughts and Tips

Let's say you buy some screws with star-shaped heads. You need to buy a star-shaped bit to match those heads. Additionally, there are different sizes of star bits, Phillips bits, etc. Make sure you get the right size, because if you don't, (a) you could strip your screws if the head of the bit is too small, or (b) the bit could be too big, which means it won't even fit into the screws, and you will be sad. One secret note: Most boxes of screws come with a tiny plastic bag containing the right bit.

IMPACT DRIVER BITS: Any bit that has a ¼″ hex shank can fit into an impact driver. It could look like any of these. Look at the bottoms—they all match, but the tops are different. The first one bores holes, the second is a hex-head driver, the third is a #3 Phillips, the fourth is a bit tip holder, and the fifth is a spade bit. Any of these will work in an impact driver. Guess what? All of them will also work in a drill.

| BIT | HEX-HEAD DRIVER | #3 PHILLIPS | BIT TIP HOLDER | SPADE BIT |

Bits that are exclusively for drills: Note the bottoms of these. They don't have that ¼″ hex shank. A drill will accept anything it can tighten its chuck around.

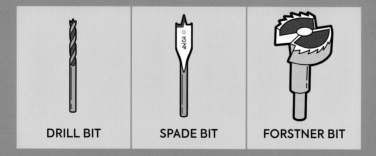

| DRILL BIT | SPADE BIT | FORSTNER BIT |

What about bit tips? Bit tips exclusively go in bit tip holders, so they can work in a drill or an impact driver.

NAIL SET

A nail set's most common job is to drive finish nails below the surface of wood far enough to allow you to cover the head of the nail with wood filler. When sanded, the wood filler blends in with the rest of the wood, and the nail becomes a mystery that only you (and all other woodworkers) know about. A nail set kind of looks like a nail, but it is made of a thicker metal, is less bendable, and has a blunt point. You can place this tip over the head of a finish nail, where it fits neatly, then hit the nail set with a hammer a few times. The nail set will push the finish nail into the wood, down below the surface. Stop hammering when the nail is about ⅛" into the wood. Don't forget to fill the hole with wood filler, let it dry, then sand it all down.

NAIL SETS

ORBITAL SANDER

An orbital sander is my personal favorite type of sander. You can get a battery-operated one, which means you can take the sander on a hike, pull a piece of wood out of your pocket ten miles away from electricity, and sand away. Totally necessary. Orbital sanders spin, rotating a round disc of sandpaper across your wood while you move the sander back and forth. The ultimate sanding experience involves a lot of circles and side to side. There are other kinds of sanders, but I think this is the best. Feel free to think your own thoughts.

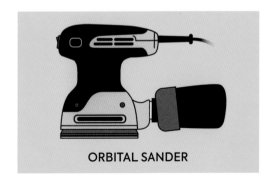

ORBITAL SANDER

PIPE WRENCH

Pipe wrenches are pretty fun. They are used to tighten and loosen pipes. Pipe wrenches are large and heavy, and they have a mechanism to rotate the very bitey teeth up and down the handle, which widens or narrows the mouth of the wrench depending on which direction you turn it. They come in a few different sizes; often you want one with a longish handle in order to maximize leverage. For most purposes, you will need two pipe wrenches, so invest in two.

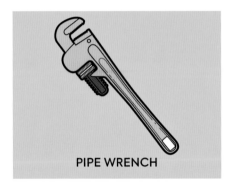

PIPE WRENCH

PLIERS

Pliers are handheld tools that grip things. There are many kinds and a few variations—some have a blunt nose and some are needle-nosed—but ultimately you use them to grip things firmly and pull.

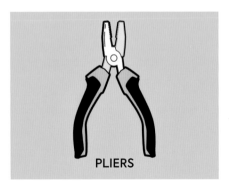

PLIERS

RULER

A regular old ruler will work just fine. So will anything with a factory-made straight edge (meaning you bought it somewhere and didn't cut the straight edge yourself).

SAW

Chop Saw (Compound Miter Saw)

A chop saw is an electric saw that accurately cuts straight, angled, and beveled cuts. The chop saw is, by far, my favorite saw. As with all these saws, you *must* learn how to operate it from someone skilled, and never use it without supervision. The chop saw allows for repeated, accurate cuts at many angles—even two angles at once, if you want to get fancy.

Handsaw

A handsaw is a saw operated with . . . your hand. No motor, no electricity. It's not for fools. Spend some time with your handsaw, practice, master the skill. Then put it in your storage cabinet and go buy a chop saw.

Jigsaw

The jigsaw is a small, handheld saw with a vertical blade that goes up and down to make its cuts. You can cut in circles with it (but not tiny circles), but you can also cut straight lines. There is generally a switch on the side that lets you adjust how versatile you want the blade. This means that if you want a straight cut, you want the blade to only move up and down in a straight line. If you are cutting in a circle, you want the blade to have the ability to turn left and right. For straight lines keep it at 0 or 1; for more circular cuts set it to 3 or 4.

There are many, many types of jigsaw blades. Just go to the hardware store and thumb through them. The thing you really want to check is the type of shank. This is how the blade attaches to the saw. The T-shaped shank is the most commonly used. If you can't remember which blade your saw takes (you can look it up online), you may want to buy both types and take them home. The next thing you want to consider when buying blades is the material you are cutting. The packaging will indicate whether it is for wood, metal, plastic, etc.

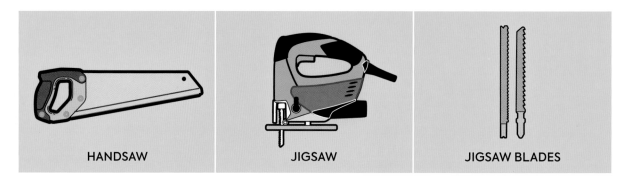

HANDSAW   JIGSAW   JIGSAW BLADES

Chop Saw vs. Compound Miter Saw

So listen. I can't send you out into the world not knowing that what I call a chop saw is technically a compound miter saw. Inevitably, some people out there will tell you that you don't know what you are talking about when you call a compound miter saw a chop saw. They are wrong. You do know what you are talking about. But technically a chop saw is an entirely different tool than what I'm talking about here. It's a beefier saw most often used to cut metal. So this person who is talking down to you is correct. But, commonly, when 98 percent of people say "chop saw," they are actually talking about a compound miter saw. I am included in that 98 percent, and I will use that term in this book. Now you know, and now you can throw some knowledgeable sass back at that know-it-all.

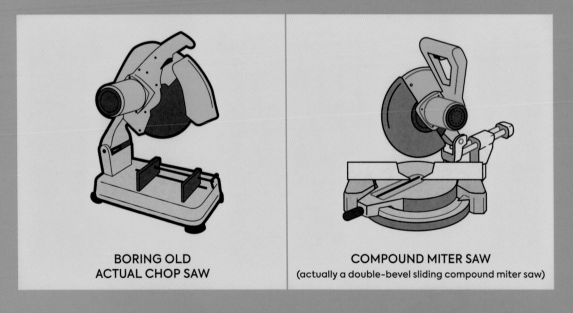

**BORING OLD
ACTUAL CHOP SAW**

COMPOUND MITER SAW
(actually a double-bevel sliding compound miter saw)

SCREWDRIVER

My recommendation for a useful screwdriver is called a six-in-one. It has a #1 and #2 Phillips bit, a #1 and #2 flathead, and two sizes of hex drivers. And guess what? It looks like a regular old screwdriver, and it doesn't cost too much.

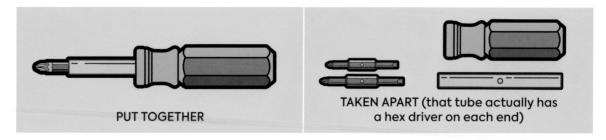

PUT TOGETHER

TAKEN APART (that tube actually has a hex driver on each end)

SPEED SQUARE

A speed square is a simple tool that looks like a triangle and is used to mark straight and angled lines accurately. You will need a sharp pencil to successfully use this tool.

TAPE MEASURE

A tape measure consists of a square metal or plastic box that has a rolled-up ruler inside. A 16′ noncheater tape is just fine for all the projects in this book. (A cheater tape has the fractions written on it. Don't worry, I go on at length about why this is a bad idea if you just keep reading.)

TROWEL OR SMALL SHOVEL

A trowel is a small, handheld shovel that can be used to dig a small hole.

WIRE SNIPS OR WIRE CUTTERS

Wire snips look like pliers, but their main purpose is to cut wire. Some pliers have a little spot at the base that will cut wire. Those will also work.

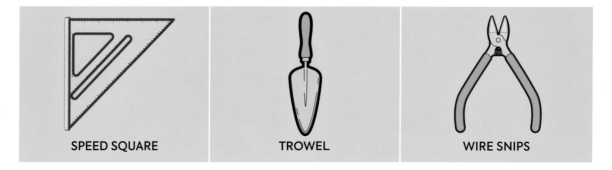

SPEED SQUARE

TROWEL

WIRE SNIPS

SKILLS

The projects in this book require some new skills that you will totally master. Here are some helpful tips to get you started.

HOW TO MEASURE

What you'll need:

- tape measure
- pencil
- paper

Reading a Tape Measure

First, you need to know the two common symbols for inch and foot. It's simple. The inch mark is ″ and the foot mark is ′. So, six inches is 6″, and six feet is 6′.

1. You will need to know how to read a tape measure. It has nothing to do with math and everything to do with memorization. Get a blank piece of paper and draw a big square U on it. This is your inch. (I'll be using abbreviations throughout the book. For example, one inch will be written as 1″, two inches will be written as 2″, etc.)

2. Now draw a line up the middle, but not quite as long as your end lines. This is your half inch. Write ½″ above it. Easy.

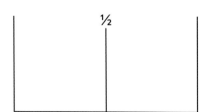

3. Halfway between the line on the left and the ½" mark, draw a line that's a little shorter than your half mark. This is your ¼". It's the very first quarter, so the top number is a one.

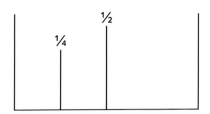

4. Halfway between the ½" and the line on the right, draw another line that is the same height as the ¼" line. This is where it gets tricky. This is the ¾" mark. Why? Because you now have four equal sections, otherwise known as quarters, and the line you just drew marks the end of the third quarter.

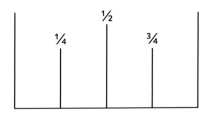

5. Quarters are easy. Think of actual quarters, like the money. If you have four quarters in real life, you have a dollar. On a tape measure, if you have four quarters, you have an inch. If you have three quarters you have . . . ¾". See? Simple. And just like with real quarters, if you had two of them, you would most likely say, "I have 50 cents"

instead of "I have two quarters." On the tape measure, you just say ½".

Now, between the first line and the ¼" line, draw one short line. This is the first eighth, otherwise known as ⅛". Again, since it's the first one, the top number is a one.

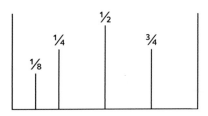

6. Skip all the way to the end, and draw another short line between the ¾" mark and the last line. This is the seventh eighth, or ⅞", which is the last eighth. This may seem confusing. I remember it this way: If you had ⅛", you would have a whole inch. So just remember that the last eighth is ⅞".

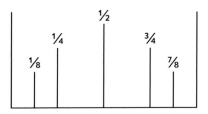

7. The only tricky measurements are the next two. Back to memorization. Draw a short little line before the ½" line. This is ⅜".

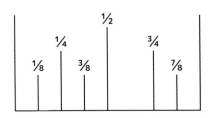

8. Now draw one after the ½" line. This is ⅝". Just remember that the eighth *before* the half inch is ⅜", and the eighth *after* the half inch is ⅝". You are so good at this!

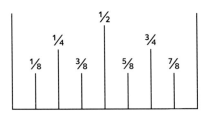

What about sixteenths, you say? Here's what I say. If you want to learn and memorize sixteenths, do it. If that feels daunting and makes you want to never pick up a tape measure, then don't. There is a technique some people use where instead of referring to the sixteenth directly, they refer to the closest measurement they do know, and use that for reference. You want the sixteenth before the ¾" mark? Say "three-quarters light." You want the one after the ¾" mark? Say "three-quarters heavy." You're so smart now—you can measure down to the sixteenth.

If I failed to convince you to skip learning sixteenths, here you go. Again, you can just memorize them by paying attention to where they are compared to the eighths. There is also some math you can do that's helpful. To start, turn the nearest quarter fraction into a sixteenth. If the nearest fraction is ¾, you would multiply the entire ¾ by ¼.

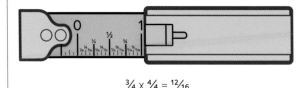

$$\frac{3}{4} \times \frac{4}{4} = \frac{12}{16}$$

You now have $\frac{12}{16}$ instead of ¾. So, if you are looking at the sixteenth before ¾, which we are now calling $\frac{12}{16}$, you know that that sixteenth is $\frac{11}{16}$ because it is one less than $\frac{12}{16}$. Math is great. A tip: If you are reading a tape measure correctly, you will never have two even numbers (like $\frac{12}{16}$). You will always have an odd number on top and an even number on the bottom. You're welcome.

Using a Tape Measure

When using a tape measure, hook the metal edge over the end of what you are measuring (the most likely scenario) or bump it up against your starting point. Pull the tape out past your measurement for the most accuracy. For example, if you are measuring to 10", pull the tape measure

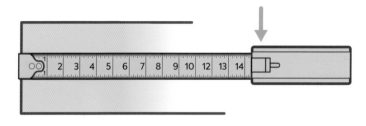

out to 14". If you are marking a measurement, continue by locking it (this usually means sliding down a button on the top of the tape measure above the spot where the tape comes out), which will free up your hands to make your crow's foot.

I have three tips for you on measuring:

1. Unless you are measuring over 12', just use inches. Why? If you use feet and inches, this is what that looks like: 4' 4¾". If you use inches only, you can just say 52¾", which is easier. It's cleaner and less confusing.

2. Sometimes you need to mark several points on one board for placement on other boards. When you are making several marks along one line, keep your tape measure on your beginning point (usually this is the edge of the wood) the entire time. So your measurements would be, say, 12", 18", 24", and 30". The poor alternative is to measure 12", then from that point measure 6", and from that point measure 6", etc. Why is this bad? I'll tell you. What if you accidentally mark one measurement wrong, then measure 6" from there? Every point thereafter will also be wrong. If you keep your tape measure positioned at one spot, then if you mess up one point, you don't mess up all of them. It's important, and a lot easier. I just taught my sister this trick and she called me smart. See, there can be many benefits to these skills, like the rare compliment from a big sister.

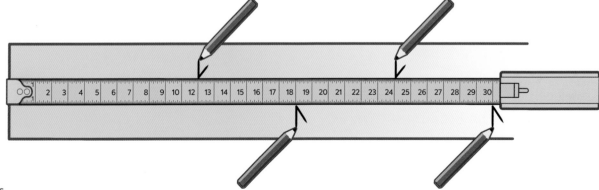

3. Let's say your project calls for five boards cut to 18″. You have a long board and you're a smart person who likes to save time. What do you do? You take your tape measure and you measure out all 18″ pieces on your board at once. You are feeling pretty smug and like you cheated the system a little, right? Well, I have bad news. Every board but your first one is going to be too short. Why? It's all about the saw blade. The saw blade has some thickness to it—about ⅛″ if you are using a chop saw, table saw, or circular saw. So what will happen? Each board after the first one will be ⅛″ short.

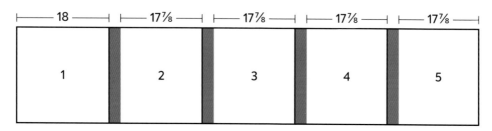

In this scenario, you would have one 18″ board, and four boards at 17⅞″ each. So instead, measure and cut one, then move on to the next. Not as fun, but more accurate.

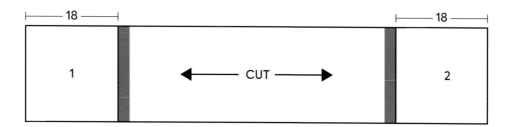

Option B? Measure from each end, cut both, and measure the next two. Please note that the cuts in this scenario are on opposite sides of the line, both on the interior part of the wood, leaving both ends at the full 18″.

Burning an Inch

The meaurements on the first inch of a tape measure are basically a waste. The tape measure hardware goes over the top of all those precious numbers you need. Let's say you need to measure ⅜″ from the edge of a piece of wood. You won't be able to see the ⅜″ line, so you want to do something called "burning an inch." Not only is it a very helpful skill; you will sound very cool tossing that

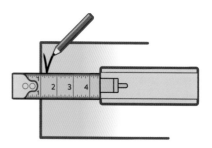

phrase around. All you do is scoot the tape measure off the edge of the piece you are measuring so that the 1″ mark sits right on the edge. Then you treat the next inch like it's the first inch, find your ⅜″ or ⅝″ or whatever number you are looking for, mark it easily, and move on.

Making a Crow's Foot

You will see the term "crow's foot" tossed around a lot in this book. The crow's foot is a really great way to mark a measurement, and you will use it on nearly every project. Sure, you can make a short, inaccurate line that will be hard to find later, or you can mark a crow's foot. A crow's foot is a V shape that looks like an arrow missing its long, straight arm. It's nice and big, and the tip of the arrow points directly at your measurement. Try it now. Yes, even if you are an adult.

To practice, you'll need a piece of paper, a pencil, and a tape measure (or ruler). Pull your tape out to around the 25″ mark, and lock it into place. This will free up both of your hands. Lay the tape measure across the piece of paper. Place the sharp tip of your pencil next to the 20″ mark on your tape measure, and draw a short line toward yourself and at an angle, making one leg of your arrow (or foot). Now place the pencil tip back at the 20″ mark, and draw another line toward yourself, but in a mirror image to your first line, forming a V. Congrats! You just drew your first crow's foot. Make sure to practice a few more times before starting on any projects. The crow's foot should be a thin, dark line.

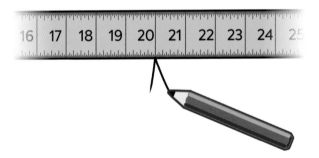

Cheater Tapes

This is important: Don't get a cheater tape. Cheater tapes are tape measures with the fractions written on them. Here's what will happen. You will use it in your garage or in your yard or in your basement shop, and you will be proud of yourself because measuring is so easy. And you'll get good at hammering nails and driving screws—so good, in fact, that friends will ask you to help them (this is one of the potential perils of becoming good at building). Anyway, you will go over to your friend's house and you'll forget your tape measure because you were bringing so many tools (your friend just has one corded drill from 1983 that she got as a hand-me-down, so . . .). After watching you dig through your tools and then finally mutter, "I forgot my tape measure," your friend says, "Oh, I have a tape measure! Hold on!" Your friend runs into the basement or garage or garden shed and pulls out a tape measure, handing it to you with a smile. And guess what? You won't be able to read it because you were using that cheater tape and thought it was just a little crutch to help you learn. It wasn't. It stole your learning, and now you are standing in your friend's yard, ready to build a fence, and you can't find ⅜". You are quite embarrassed.

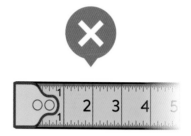

Moral? Don't buy a cheater tape.

HOW TO USE A SPEED SQUARE

Speed squares are super interesting and can be very helpful when marking lines. The speed square allows you to draw a straight line at many angles. The most helpful and common angle is the 90-degree angle—a straight line across the board. To use a speed square accurately, first, spend a little time practicing how to place it on the wood. Hang the wider edge over the edge of the wood, tucking it really tightly against the wood. Keeping it tight against the wood is the only way to get a straight line.

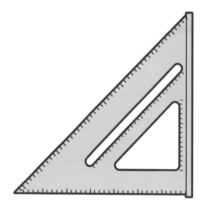

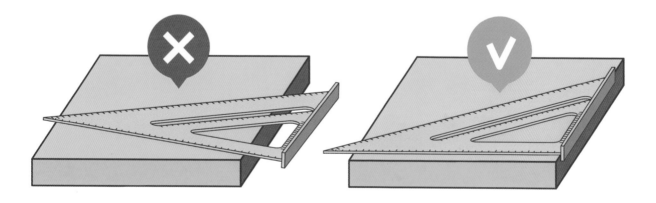

You also want to make sure that the majority of the square is on the wood. If not, the square can become wobbly and your line will be crooked.

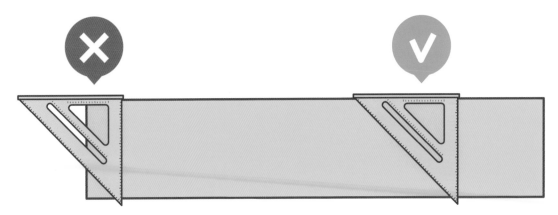

To do the projects in this book, you need to know how to draw two different lines across a piece of wood: a 90-degree line and a 45-degree line. These are both great to use when you are cutting wood, especially if you are using a jigsaw or circular saw. Knowing how to mark a 45-degree angle helps when using the chop saw as well.

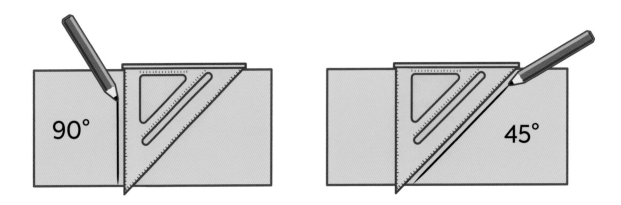

There is a lot more to explore about the speed square, including how to draw every angle between 0 and 90, and how to draw roof angles. For this book, you don't need those extra numbers, but if you feel like exploring, you can read the manual that comes with some speed squares, or you can hop on the internet.

Drawing a Line Through
a Crow's Foot with a Speed Square

Place the tip of your pencil on your crow's foot. (See "Making a Crow's Foot" earlier in this chapter for how to draw a crow's foot.) Holding it in place, place your speed square on the wood, wide part over the long edge, and slide it toward your crow's foot until it touches your pencil. Holding the speed square in place, pick up the pencil, place it at the top of the board, and run the pencil along the edge of your speed square, pressing firmly to get a solid line. Do not repeat this motion to make your line darker, as tempting as that is. Although remarking it over and over will make it darker, it will also make it wider. You want a thin, dark line—thin being an imperative word. Remember: The wide part of the speed square hangs over the long edge of the board, and stays nice and *snug* against the board.

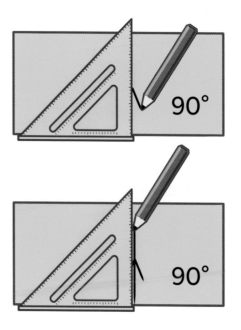

Measuring Along a Line
You Drew with Your Speed Square

So, you've drawn a line with your speed square, and now the directions tell you to "measure along this line." This is easy enough. Take your tape measure, hook the metal end of the tape measure tightly over the end of the board, and pull the tape measure out so it is parallel and on one side of your speed square line. Look for the measurement you need, and draw a crow's foot at that point. You might need to draw a few points, so leave your tape measure in place and keep drawing crow's feet.

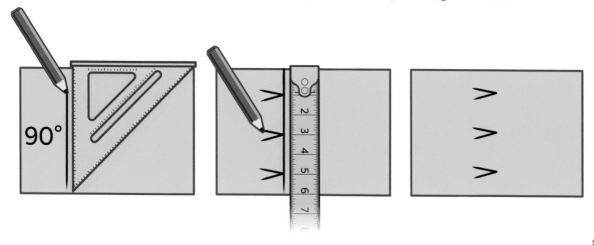

How to Make Something Square (Squaring a Box)

You want to make sure the things you build are square. *Square* is a technical term meaning each corner is a 90-degree angle. I could explain why, but for now, just trust me. To find out if your project is square, you want to measure across it diagonally in both directions. Hook one end of the tape measure on one corner, pull diagonally across to the other corner, and look at the measurement. Now do this with the other two corners. If the numbers match, you are an expert. If not, let's fix it. First, figure out which measurement is longer. Place one finger on each of the corners corresponding to the longer measurement, and push them toward each other. Did that work? If not, you might need a hammer and clamps. Try tapping the same spots with a hammer. If this doesn't work, place a clamp on those same points and twist to tighten. Remember, you can't do this if you have already heavily secured the project with screws or nails. How do you know when your project is square? Keep measuring diagonally. When your numbers match, it's square. You can move on to the next step.

HOW TO DRILL

What you'll need:

- screwdriver
- cordless power drill and/or impact driver
- drill bit set

Quick Note: Using a Screwdriver

Although most people use drills and impact drivers, screwdrivers have not been replaced. They are great for small projects like hanging a picture on a wall, or for simple repairs.

When using a screwdriver, just remember to turn it slowly, and keep applying pressure, whether you are driving or removing a screw. The best way to avoid stripping a screw is to keep that pressure on it!

Parts of a Drill

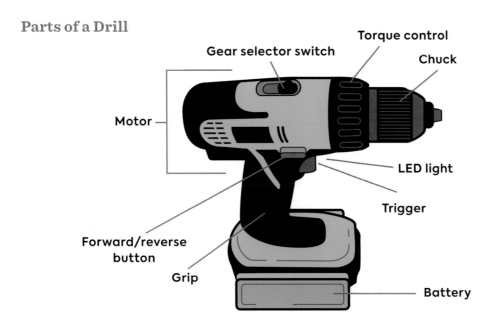

There are a lot of buttons and numbers on a drill. The front end of the drill has a bunch of numbers on it going around in a full circle, and then one picture of a drill bit.

Here's what you need to know: You should use the setting with the picture of the drill bit. The numbers don't control speed—for the most part, the trigger does (more on that later). The only time I have used those numbers with real purpose is when installing drywall. Adjusting the numbers allows you to change the torque (power) of the drill, meaning you can adjust the amount of resistance the drill will withstand before stopping. For most projects, you won't need to use those number settings.

There is often a sliding gear shift on the top of the drill. This is actually very handy. You have two options, 1 or 2. In first gear, your speed is slower but your torque is higher. This means the power is going toward spinning the screw when it meets resistance. If you are drilling into a hard wood, switching to first gear would be helpful. If you are drilling into something soft, you might as well switch to second gear, which will force the drill to spend energy on speed instead of turning the screw against resistance. One trick: If your battery is low, you can switch to second gear, which will give you a short boost of battery power.

Getting Started Drilling

When using a drill, first check that your clothes are not loose and that no hoodie strings, bracelets, necklaces, head gear, or hair is hanging down in front of you. These are unsafe near the rotating parts of the drill.

Some people wear gloves when using a drill. I don't, and I believe that gloves are a safety hazard, as they can get caught in the twisting motion of the drill. If you choose to wear gloves, make sure they fit very tightly while still allowing for mobility.

Installing a Drill Bit Like a Boss

Okay, so this is tricky, and I want you to focus. Because if you can do this, you will impress everyone. You ready?

First, put the drill in forward (as opposed to reverse), and make sure the end of the drill is open: When you look at it face on, is there a hole big enough for your bit? That's what you are looking for.

Grab a Phillips-head bit that is in a bit tip holder. Hold the bit tip holder between your pointer finger and thumb, roughly in the middle lengthwise. Slide the smooth end into the open end of the drill, holding it in a hover position in the middle. Take your remaining fingers and wrap them around the chuck of the drill. Hold on tight with these three fingers.

Next, with your other hand, *gently* touch the trigger. What's about to happen is that the drill is going to start closing in on the bit. This is where you might lose faith in yourself. *You can do this.* The important part is to keep that trigger finger light, and the three fingers holding the chuck very tight. Soon you will hear a quick "click click click." That's how you know you're done and your bit is in. If your bit is crooked, place the drill in reverse, hold the bit and chuck like you have been holding them, and hit the trigger just a little. Now put the drill back in forward, and try again. You will get it! To take it out like a boss, place the drill in reverse, hold on to the chuck—no need to hold the bit—and hit the trigger lightly. The drill will open right up and let loose your bit. Congrats! Also, you should probably practice a little.

Should You Use an Impact Driver, or a Drill?

Here's the truth. For most of your projects, an impact driver is the tool for you. It gives you more power behind your work. The only time you need a drill is if the bit you are using won't actually fit in an impact driver, meaning it doesn't have that ¼" hex shank. What I usually do if I am working on a project that requires driving screws and boring holes is to put the boring (twist bit) bit in my drill, and the driving bit in my impact driver. This saves time and maximizes each tool's power.

Driving a Screw

1. Please note that there is a neutral—an area between forward and reverse where the trigger will not compress. This is good to remember for that moment you think your drill is broken—it's not. It's just in neutral.

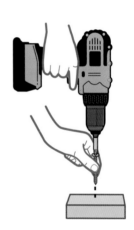

2. Make sure your drill is in the forward position and you have loaded the proper bit. Take your dominant hand and place your pointer finger on the trigger, wrapping the rest of your fingers around the handle, sometimes called a grip. Your nondominant hand will be used at first to hold the screw in place. While the drill is still in the air, place the screw onto the bit, then place the tip of the screw onto the wood where you want it to go in. Hold the screw lightly, then hit the trigger, also lightly. One cool thing about drills and impact drivers is that they have feather triggers. This means that if you pull the trigger lightly, the drill will go slowly. If you pull it all the way, it will go incredibly fast. We're going to start slowly. Apply downward pressure with your dominant hand, and hit the trigger lightly. You want the screw to be pushing down as it turns—this is important.

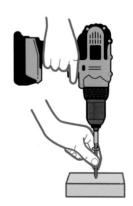

3. As soon as the screw bites the wood, meaning that it can stand in the wood on its own without moving, move your nondominant hand to the

top/back of the drill, behind the motor housing, and push down hard while keeping that trigger finger light. This is a key skill, and I know you can do it. It's tempting to pull hard on that trigger, but resist. The downward pressure keeps the bit and the screw tightly connected. If they disconnect, you will strip the screw. Stripping a screw means that you will begin to hollow out the area where the drill and screw meet, making your drilling less effective with each turn until you completely strip it and the screw is stuck and you feel a little sheepish. If you are using a drill, you will know you are stripping a screw because it will make a

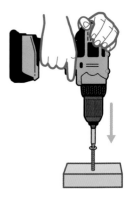

"pop pop pop" noise. On an impact driver, it's a little harder to hear, because the impact driver also makes a similar (but not the same) noise. (Note: To remove a stripped screw, get a pair of vise-grips pliers and turn the screw backward until it comes out. If things get dire, you can actually get a drill bit the same size as your screw and drill through the screw.)

4. To back a screw out of a piece of wood, first make absolutely sure that the correct bit is in the drill. Next, place your hands where you had them at the end of step 3—behind the motor housing and on the handle, with your index finger on the trigger. Put the drill in reverse. With the hand behind the motor housing, press down hard. This is where many people end up stripping a screw. In the beginning of removing a screw, you must push down as hard as, if not harder than, you did to put the screw in. Press the trigger very lightly, and slowly ease the screw out, while pushing down hard on the drill itself.

Tip: When you are boring a hole, you don't need to switch to reverse in order to take the bit out of the wood. Keep your finger on the trigger and simply pull up and out. Boring in and then pulling out in one motion is very common and more efficient.

Using an Impact Driver

Impact drivers are great tools that are often confused with drills. They have a shorter nose and are designed for driving screws more efficiently than a drill. They hammer the screw in as it turns. This makes driving a screw much easier, especially for younger kids (but every adult secretly, and often openly, prefers to drive screws with an impact driver because it's simpler and quicker). The impact driver is much louder than a drill;

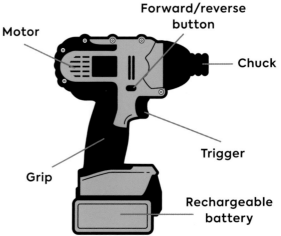

Motor

Forward/reverse button

Chuck

Trigger

Grip

Rechargeable battery

as it drives the screw, it makes a noisy "tap tap tap" sound that some find unnerving, so have earplugs handy. The sound is similar to the sound a drill or driver makes when stripping a screw, so learn to hear the difference. My campers learn the difference because when I hear a screw being stripped anywhere within 100' of me, I start yelling, "That's the bad noise! That's the bad noise!" until they let go of the trigger. You can find someone who will yell this for you, or you can just train your ear.

¼" HEX SHANKS

Note: To use an impact driver, you need a bit that has a base that looks like these (see illustration).

To install a bit, you either pull the sleeve on the nose (the collet) of the impact driver back and slide the bit in, then release the sleeve, or you simply push the bit into the impact driver, depending upon the model. Try both ways. Give the bit a little tug to make sure it is in securely. To release the bit, simply pull the sleeve out again. Watch out—on newer impact drivers, the bit will jump out of the impact driver a little, and it could fall to the ground.

Purchasing tip: Since the invention of the impact driver, drills have become very cheap, and for the most part you can buy a drill and driver set together for what people used to pay for a drill alone. I recommend getting the set.

Predrilling Holes (Pilot Holes)

Predrilling a hole where you want to drive a screw can make driving that screw a little easier. Another benefit: If you want to drive a screw near the edge of a board, predrilling a hole prevents cracking the board. Using a bit that is smaller than your screw, you create a path for the screw. A ¹⁄₁₆" or ⅛" bit works for most common screws—you don't want to go any bigger, or your screw won't have any wood to catch as it goes in.

Practice: Use your tape measure to measure out a random spot on a piece of wood, maybe between 6" and 10". Mark a crow's foot. Place a ⅛" bit into your drill, and bore a hole right on your mark. Easy. Note that the ¹⁄₁₆" bit is very useful for predrilling, but it breaks easily.

Toenailing

Toenailing is when you connect two boards with a nail or screw at an angle. Some people say "toe-screw" when you are using a screw, but I find that a little clunky, so I use the much less clunky phrase "toenail with a screw" or "use a screw to toenail." Your choice! Why would you do this? It's a nice and easy way to connect two boards that are coming together to make a corner when you can't access the end of one board. It's also great when you want to connect two pieces that are too thick to connect the regular way. You might not understand everything about toenailing now, but there will come a time when toenailing is just the thing you need. This is how it works:

Line your boards up the way you want them to end up. You might need someone to hold them for you, or use clamps to hold them in place. When you are toenailing, there can be some movement, so you constantly want to check that your boards are where you want them to end up. When you are using a screw, it's best to predrill the hole first. To do that, use a 1/16" or 1/8" bit. In fact, if you feel more comfortable, you can also predrill with a 1/16" bit before you drive in a nail, and your accuracy will be much better. Pre-drill at the angle you need to catch both boards. Start your screw or nail straight, like you normally would.

When the screw/drill bit or nail barely catches, turn it to the angle you need. Continue to nail or screw it at that angle, making sure your boards line up.

Using a Drill Press

A drill press is a machine that sits either on your workbench or on the ground (if you get a tall one). Instead of using your hands to direct a drill, the drill press lets you lower and raise a bit to bore holes to your exact preference, either straight or angled. This might be a tool to invest in, way down the road; for now, it's good to know it's out there.

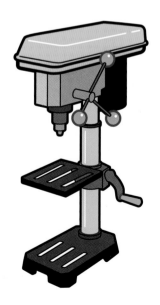

Drill vs. Drill Press?

A drill is a handheld power tool that bores holes. A drill press is a large stationary tool. The drill press is generally safer for larger bits and is more precise when you are looking for a perfectly vertical hole.

HOW TO SAW

What you'll need:

- handsaw
- chop saw and/or jigsaw (with an adult's supervision)
- Possibly a sturdy power cord

Saws are used to cut wood. There are many kinds. The two you will need most often to complete the projects in this book are a chop saw and a jigsaw. But depending on your age, you could venture into the wider world of saws by learning how to use a table saw, circular saw, and Sawzall (technically known as a reciprocating saw, and another favorite of mine). For any of these saws, the best way to learn is to find the most safety-minded person you know who has used a saw for years and ask them to teach you. If they don't start by putting on safety glasses and ear protection, maybe find someone else.

Here's the deal. Most of these saws can very severely injure you, and you don't want to mess around with that. Especially the circular saw and table saw. Do not try to use these saws alone; do not learn to use them from your phone. Do not try with an unskilled friend. Take a class, or learn from someone who is a professional—and has all their fingers.

What Saw to Use?

In this book, I talk a lot about the chop saw and jigsaw, and I often give you the option to use either. (See page 22 for more about these different saws.) For the most part, the chop saw is more accurate and makes a nicer cut. If you haven't been trained on the chop saw, though, using the jigsaw is a great way to get started on these projects. It is a safer and simpler saw, but you still need to learn how to use it from a skilled adult.

If you use a jigsaw, your cuts will not necessarily be beautiful. You may not show them off to your friends. But you will accomplish the task and create a project that you will definitely be proud of.

Safe Cutting Techniques

You need to learn how to use saws from an actual person who has a lot of experience. Once you have, here are some things to keep in mind:

1. Always use ear protection and safety glasses that fit you well.

2. Always keep your fingers well away from the blade.

3. The board you are cutting needs to be secure and longer than 6″. If you are using a jigsaw, the board should be clamped (see page 46). On the chop saw, the board should be pushed against the fence. (The flat part of the chop saw, where you set the wood, is called the table. The part that is connected to it, perpendicular and behind it, is called the fence.)

4. Never, never start the blade while it is touching the wood.

5. When using a chop saw, keep your arms parallel to the blade. If you adjust the angle of the blade, move your arms to keep them parallel to the blade.

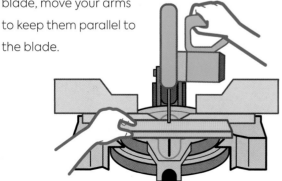

6. When using a chop saw, never, ever cross your arms.

7. Your clothes should be on the tighter side. Loose sleeves, tops, etc., can get caught in blades.

8. Get rid of necklaces, sweatshirt strings, and bracelets. Tie your hair back, into a bun if necessary. You don't want anything loose or hanging.

9. Keep your feet in a wide stance, preferably with one foot comfortably behind the other, so that if you were pushed off balance your back foot would catch you. Do not stand with your feet together and side by side.

10. Make sure the area around you is clear of people and objects. Do not be afraid to tell someone to move away to give you space. You want zero distractions while using a saw. Make sure you are not backed into a corner or have a wall behind you. You want plenty of room for your body to move as necessary if something goes awry.

11. Take your time. You are not in a rush and have nothing to prove. You will never regret double-checking for safety and slowing down to remain focused.

Avoid Cutting Between Two Support Points

When you are cutting wood with a handsaw, jigsaw, or circular saw, you want the wood to fall freely to the ground. Another way to put this is that you don't want to cut between two points. For example, if you set up two sawhorses and laid a 2x4 across them so you could cut it, the sawhorses are two points. In this scenario, you have already measured, marked a crow's foot, and drawn a line with a speed square. That line should not be *between* the sawhorses, but on the outside of them. To make the cut, you would be standing on the outside of the sawhorses, not between them. If you cut between two points, like sawhorses, the wood will bind the blade of the saw, meaning that both pieces of wood will kind of fall in and grab the blade of the saw. Not only will this mess up your cut, but it's dangerous. Double-check every time to ensure that you are letting the wood fall freely to the ground.

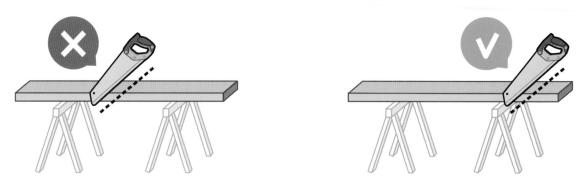

Cutting Close to a Stable Surface

To cut wood correctly with a jigsaw or other similar saw, make sure the wood is hanging off the end of a stable surface. To minimize vibration of the wood while cutting, which is unsafe, you want to clamp or hold the wood so the cutting point of the saw blade is close to a stable surface.

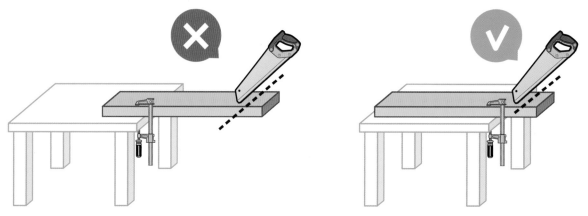

HOW TO HAMMER

First, put on safety glasses. To hammer correctly, hold the nail in your nondominant hand. Then, holding the hammer about halfway down the handle with your dominant hand, tap lightly but solidly on the nail. Once the nail is secured in the wood—meaning you can't bump it over easily—move your nondominant hand out of the way (it can hold the wood down from about a foot away), slide your dominant hand down to the very end of the handle, and tap that nail harder. You want to hold the hammer at the top, you say? Up by the hammer head? *Stop it.* Holding it there will make your hammering less accurate, and by the end of the project your hand will be so sore. Using the hammer that way is like punching the nail instead of using the hammer to do the work.

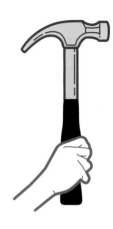

Speaking of sore hands, hammering is a whole-arm activity. Stop and check to see how you are doing it. Are you just moving your wrist? Moving your elbow but keeping your wrist straight? Your swing should start at the shoulder and move through your elbow and wrist. Using your whole arm will cause you to hit the nail very hard, making your hits more efficient. When I was learning to hammer well, my boss Ray told me not to worry about the number of times I missed, but when I did hit that nail, it should be significant. So, if you miss, don't worry. Just keep practicing. Preferably on junk wood.

Cat's Paw:
The Hammer's Best Friend

The cat's paw is a tool used to remove nails, and it's maybe my second-favorite tool. A cat's paw (no, not a cat's *claw*) is used to remove nails fully embedded in wood. To use a cat's paw, you must have a hammer.

1. Stand the cat's paw next to the embedded nail, so the stem of the tool is parallel to the nail.

2. Angle the claw portion under the nail, and hammer the back end.

$3.$ As you hammer on the cat's paw, pull the handle down toward the wood, while continuing to hammer. (Some people forget that part! Keep hammering away!)

$4.$ The nail should slowly be inching out of the wood. When enough of the nail head is sticking above the surface of the wood, feel free to slide the hammer claw under the nail head to finish the job.

HOW TO CLAMP

Clamps are like an extra set of hands, but often more secure. Clamps can hold wood firmly on your work surface while you cut, or they can tighten two glued pieces together while the glue dries. Clamps can also help you square up a small project, or force a piece of wood to move in a way that a hammer can't. There are a few types of clamps, and most likely the clamp you are thinking of is a C-clamp.

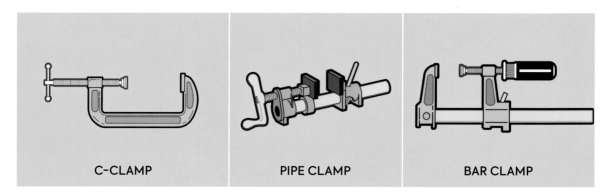

| C-CLAMP | PIPE CLAMP | BAR CLAMP |

Pipe clamps and bar clamps are essentially the same, but pipe clamps tend to be longer and are used in more professional wood shops. Bar clamps are smaller and are perfectly great for any project you are working on from this book.

Bar clamps and pipe clamps use the same system to tighten two or three or a million things together. Here's how to use them. First, make sure the piece that twists is all the way open. Next, apply pressure to the small metal piece, called the spring lock trigger.

Applying pressure to the spring lock trigger will allow you to slide the movable arm up and down the pipe or bar. With your wood or metal placed between the two arms, slide the arms together. Once they're tight, it's time to twist. Begin turning the only piece that twists until you can turn no more. Check your pieces of wood—they should be nearly immobile. To release, simply twist the handle in the opposite direction until it is loose, then press the spring lock trigger to fully remove the clamp.

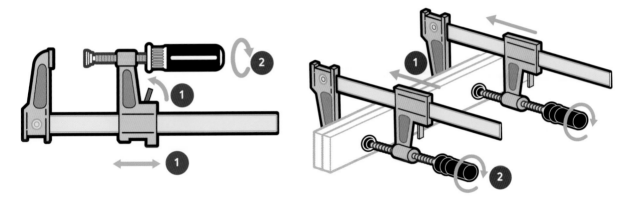

HOW TO USE
A PIPE WRENCH

To use a pipe wrench, you must place the mouth of the wrench around the pipe, tighten it, and rotate the wrench around the pipe. Here's the thing—the wrench will grab the pipe if it is rotating in one direction, but it won't grab the pipe while rotating in the other. If the wrench doesn't grab as you rotate it, take it off the pipe, turn it over, and try again. In most scenarios, you will have one pipe wrench on one piece of your project, and the other pipe wrench on a separate pipe. Whether you are tightening or loosening, you will want to work the two wrenches in opposite directions to get the job done.

THE GIRLS AND THEIR PROJECTS

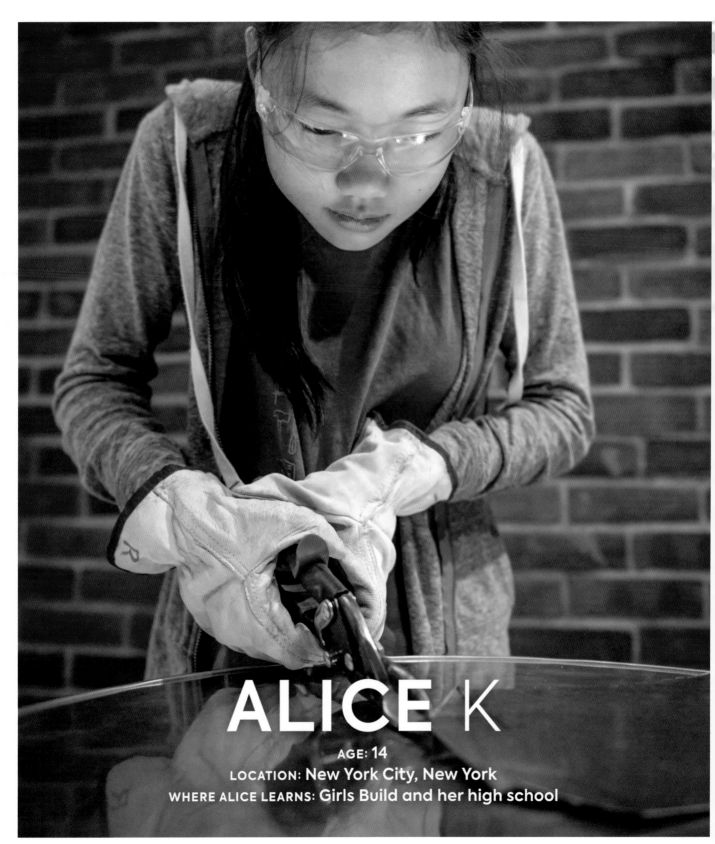

ALICE K

AGE: 14
LOCATION: New York City, New York
WHERE ALICE LEARNS: Girls Build and her high school

> *I build because I like the feeling of accomplishing something.*
> *It makes me feel proud when I can say, 'I made that.'*

What are some things you want us to know about you?

I like to build, design layouts for buildings, sew, and write stories. I also care a lot about animals, which is why I want to become a vet when I grow up.

What is the first thing you ever built?

In my preschool, there was a woodworking station, and my uncle would come help me build anything I wanted. I remember making a wooden car and painting it. I built it because I liked to play around with toy cars. Something about making my own toys seemed unusual and intriguing.

How does building make you feel?

Building makes me feel proud when I finish making something.

Why do you build?

I build because I like the feeling of accomplishing something. It makes me feel proud when I can say, "I made that."

What advice do you have for other girls?

When building something, it can be frustrating when you get one measurement wrong and you have to redo the project, but in the end it's worth it. I built a metal lunchbox at camp and since I was the first one to finish, we had to estimate where the clip would go. We redid that five to six times until we finally got it in the right place. Now I get compliments on it, and they don't even notice the mistakes! So my advice would be to not give up when building something.

What is the first step in trying something new?

I think the first step in trying something new is to be open-minded. When I went to camp, I was surprised when we didn't just do woodworking. Instead, we also did metalwork and more. Yet I kept an open mind, and all the projects turned out well.

Who do you look up to?

I look up to my parents a lot because they are hardworking. If I want to become a vet, I would need to go to graduate school after college for some years. This means that to achieve my goals, I need to work hard. I push myself quite hard sometimes, but I know how to have fun too. I want to grow up and be able to enjoy my job and have a family. That all would require hard work though.

What other activities make you feel courageous, strong, and bold?

I enjoy parkour, acro-gymnastics, and anything in that section. Not many girls do parkour, so it makes me feel strong. I also feel courageous, since I'm taking a chance in it. Acro-gymnastics makes me feel courageous and strong too. To be lifted up into the air and to do stunts is sometimes scary but also thrilling. But I'd have to say that parkour is more unusual, so when I do it, it makes me feel even more courageous than I would be when I do acro-gymnastics.

What are some ideas of things girls can build at home?

At home, girls can build wooden structures and maybe do some metalwork. If they have the equipment, they can hammer or drill some pieces of wood together into whatever they desire. If they have the equipment used for bending metal, they can make all sorts of items, like a pencil case.

What project are you sharing with us?

A sheet metal pencil box.

CLAIRE

AGE: 12
LOCATION: Port Townsend, Washington
**WHERE CLAIRE LEARNS: The Girls Boat program
at Northwest Maritime Center**

> *Be okay with messing up . . .*
> *The worst mistake you can make is giving up.*

What are some things you want us to know about you?

I live by Fort Worden, and I go up and explore a lot in bunkers and in the trees. I love playing cello and snowboarding. I lived in Fiji when I was little, from one year old to five years old, and we lived on a boat. I loved swimming and snorkeling, and I loved catching hermit crabs and skinks. I love coconut and vara, which is the sprout of a coconut. I am an only child. I have asthma, which means in PE or anything I have to stop running if my asthma gets triggered. My asthma is triggered by running and dust, so I have to wear a face mask in a wood shop or other dusty place. I had an asthma attack when I was in third or fourth grade, and I had to go to the emergency room because I couldn't breathe, but I think my asthma is getting better.

What is the first thing you ever built?

In Fiji, I turned the husk of a coconut into a boat, made a mast out of a stick, and used a leaf for the sail. I also made sand-castle houses for hermit crabs.

How does building make you feel?

Building makes me feel accomplished, happy, and satisfied. You use scraps of wood and it, step by step, turns into something you can use around the house.

Why do you build?

You get to make something useful that's homemade, which makes it extra special.

What advice do you have for other girls?

Be okay with messing up. When you start a project you have to realize you might mess up, or it won't actually work. But then you can fix the mistakes you made the first time, and then it works! The worst mistake you can make is giving up.

What's the first step in trying something new?

You have to know that it might not work the first time, and you have to be okay with that. Failure is proof that you are trying.

Who do you look up to?

I look up to my mom and dad because they are so amazing and strong and powerful. My mom just does everything. She does work, she braids my hair every day, she makes me breakfast, and helps me with homework. My dad is really athletic and tries to get me biking and kitesurfing. If I don't want to do something, he doesn't give up. Like snowboarding—at first I didn't like it, but now I love it!

What are some other activities that make you feel courageous, strong, and bold?

Snowboarding. You are trying things new all the time, like a new jump, and you fall. Then the next time you get a tiny bit in the air, and you feel really satisfied with yourself. In snowboarding you are always trying something new, and always falling down. Also, I just started cello this year and I have come so far. One more thing is climbing trees—you are on tiny branches and you can touch the top, and then you can see everything, the hills, the town, and you feel really big and powerful!

What are some ideas of things girls can build at home?

I build fairy houses a lot, and you can build a whole world— wells, ladders, elevators, places to sleep. I built a shelter for my chickens, which was just two sawhorses with plywood over the top; then I got their old feed bags and stapled those to the sawhorses. That way when it was rainy it could keep them dry, and when it was sunny they could dust bathe.

What project are you sharing with us?

My airplane. I made it when I was in third grade in my woodworking class.

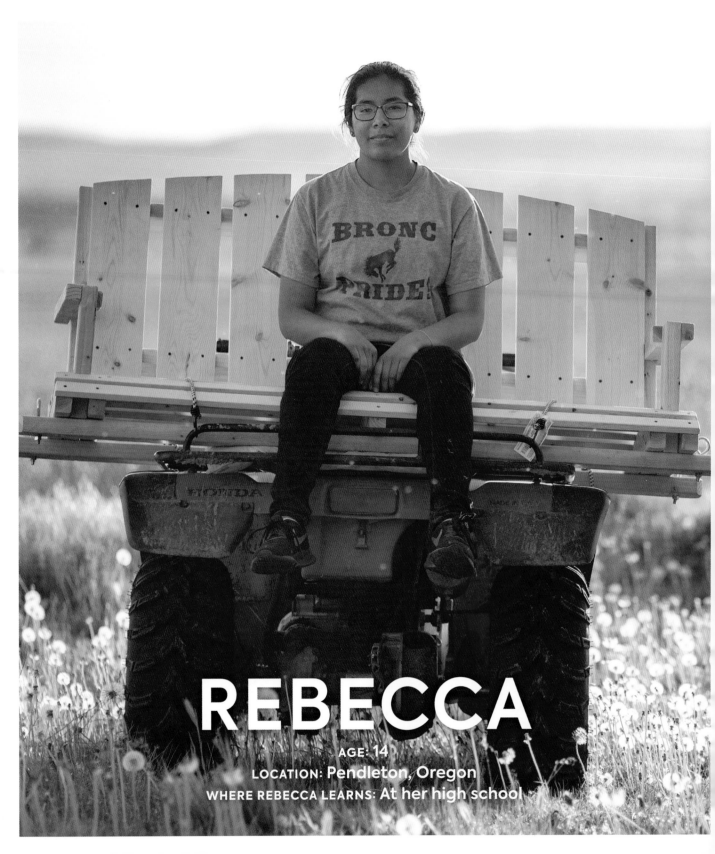

REBECCA

AGE: 14
LOCATION: Pendleton, Oregon
WHERE REBECCA LEARNS: At her high school

> *The first thing I ever made in shop was a sanding block—no power tools. It took forever!*

What are some things you want us to know about you?

I am an enrolled member of the confederated tribes of the Umatilla Indian reservation. I am proud to be Native. We come from strong people and I was taught that we, too, can be strong. And that I can be anything I want to be and that our heritage is very important. I've been doing wood shop since seventh grade. I'm in eighth grade now. I started playing violin in fourth grade, and I've been playing since then. I'm very shy about it though. There is something about music I am really drawn to. It helps me destress, just like woodworking does. I have two sisters and six brothers and I am the second youngest. I like living out here because in the city there are more people and it's crowded and loud. It's nicer to calm down, quiet down. When I have downtime, I read a little bit, sometimes on a nice day on my porch. I like to drive the four-wheeler around when I'm allowed. When the horses were here I would take them and go riding in the back field. I'm also in 4-H with my dog Kayah and with my horse.

What is the first thing you ever built?

The first thing I remember building was my pallet tray. I used to play with Legos a little bit too. Last year I built picnic tables for outdoor school. And actually, the first thing I ever made in shop was a sanding block—no power tools. It took forever!

How does building make you feel?

It makes me feel useful—like when we do community projects. I can give back, instead of building just for me. I like to destress a little bit, and it's kinda nice to do my own thing sometimes.

Why do you build?

Well, when they gave us the option in seventh grade, it was something different that I'd never done. I was already interested in engines, and I'd watch people build stuff. I'd think, "That seems cool, that seems interesting." Being Native, we need to pass down traditions so we don't lose them. For me, being artistic and working with my hands to create something new gives me power. I am proud to share these creations with other people.

What advice do you have for other girls?

Be who you want to be. Don't let others tell you who you have to be. You don't have to be that girly girl with the makeup and hair. You can be wild and crazy. You can really just be you. Definitely do what you want to do, but don't completely defy what you're told. You don't have to be out-of-control wild, but you don't have to be completely quiet and calm.

What's the first step in trying something new?

You should probably be open-minded to the possibilities. It's like trying a new food. You might not like the way it sounds or smells. Keep your mind open, and be ready for different tastes. You might like it.

Who do you look up to?

I'd have to say my mom. She is fifty now and getting her degree. She is a single mother and she really doesn't ask for other people's help raising us. She's very headstrong. She may not be the most confident in how she does things, but she definitely makes a big impact on my life. She has definitely helped me through my fourteen years a lot.

What are some other activities that make you feel courageous, strong, and bold?

Definitely playing the violin. Sometimes I'll just be messing around and I make a good sound with it and I feel like I did something, and I'm proud of myself for that, instead of having to play what's right in front of me. When I'm out in the shop playing by myself, that's when I get my loudest because no one is around to listen. And I feel pretty confident. And I feel good.

What are some ideas of things girls can build at home?

There's a lot of stuff. The porch swing, or a mirror, or really if you can find the right instructions, or be creative on your own, you can really make anything.

What project are you sharing with us?

My wooden porch swing. Me and my friend Leah helped each other build them.

ALICE S

AGE: 9
LOCATION: Portland, Oregon
WHERE ALICE LEARNS: Girl Scouts and at school

> *Sometimes [building] can be hard and frustrating, but in the end you get to make something you can be really proud of.*

What are some things you want us to know about you?

I like to play games, read, and build. My favorite games to play are Minecraft, chess, and checkers. I take circus class, where I go on the trapeze, trampoline, and silks. My favorite trick to do is the drop on the silks. I also do Girl Scouts. I've learned outdoor skills, like making food by the campfire and how to make crafts with nature. We even have gone on overnight campouts, which have been my favorite activity. I live with my sister, Willa (she does circus too), my mommy, daddy, and goldendoodle, Sandy.

What is the first thing you ever built?

I built a gingerbread house out of graham crackers, candy, and frosting. It was really messy but tasted good! It had four walls and a roof.

How does building make you feel?

It makes me feel calm, happy, very interested in my project, and proud.

Why do you build?

It is fun and I learn new things.

What advice do you have for other girls?

Don't give up on what you are building. Sometimes it can be hard and frustrating, but in the end you get to make something you can be really proud of.

What's the first step in trying something new?

I would go on the computer and look up what I want to learn about. I can also check out books from my library and learn as much as I can about it!

Who do you look up to?

My third grade teacher, Ms. Lee. She is my favorite teacher I've had so far, and I've had some really amazing teachers. She has taught me to push myself and do my best when the work is hard. She even goes to school after teaching all day! She does special projects for our class, like teaching us how to make piñatas, how to build gingerbread houses, and how to make hot chocolate!

What other activities make you feel courageous, bold, and strong?

Reading, cooking, and writing. Writing makes me feel bold because it shows my creativity. I can write about my favorite places. I like to cook because I get to create meals. It is fun to mix ingredients together to transform into something yummy.

What are some ideas of things girls can build at home?

An outside mud kitchen! You can make it with old kitchen materials, like a sink, bowls, spatulas, whisks, pots, and pans. You can also make a cool fort. One time, we made one with lots of sheets and it had multiple rooms. We kept it up for a long time to play in.

What project are you sharing with us?

I built a chicken ladder for the chickens on the farm.

ALICE'S CHICKEN LADDER

Alice and her sister, Willa, built a chicken ladder at a friend's farm for their new chicken coop. The girls used some basic tools for a quick project. It was cold outside, but Alice was a trooper through and through, wanting to finish the project and watch those chickens walk into the coop. The beauty of this project is that chickens don't care how straight their ramp steps are, so you can use a square, or you can eyeball it. Have fun!

MATERIALS

❏ One 2x10 or 2x12, about 6' long (for an average coop)

❏ 12 pieces of lath 12" long each

❏ 24 exterior nails, 1" to 1½" long (your choice)

❏ Two 3" exterior screws (to attach ladder to chicken coop)

TOOLS

❏ Tape measure

❏ Pencil

❏ Speed square (optional)

❏ Hammer

❏ Handsaw, if lath pieces are longer than the width of your board

❏ Drill or impact driver

SKILLS

❏ Measuring

❏ Hammering

❏ Sawing (if needed)

❏ Drilling (to install the ladder)

Adult oversight:

Cost after tools:

Safety gear:
• Safety glasses

Work surface:
Fairly flat

Skill level:

Time:

STEPS

1. Put on safety glasses and ear protection. Check for and remove loose clothing and jewelry, and make sure hair is tied back.

2. Lay your 2x10 or 2x12 on flat ground or on a workbench. (We are going to call it a 2x10 throughout the instructions for simplicity's sake, but if you are using a 2x12, just sub a 2x12 where it says 2x10.)

3. Measure 6" from the narrow end of the board, and mark a crow's foot (see page 30 for crow's foot instructions). Using your speed square, draw a line through the crow's foot as long as the speed square (see page 31 for how to use a speed square). This will be the rough

guide for nailing your lath. If you don't have a speed square, lay a piece of lath across and eyeball it to see if it looks straight.

4. Grab a piece of lath (a narrow, thin strip of wood), your hammer, and two nails.

5. Lay the lath along your line so the long edge of your lath touches your pencil line. If your lath is longer than the board is wide, it's okay. Make sure that the two boards are flush on one edge. Start hammering a nail into the lath about 3" from the edge of the wood, making sure not to hit your finger. Once the nail is secured into the lath but not into the 2x10, check and make sure the lath is still on your line, and that the lath and

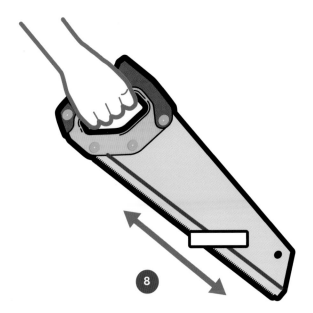

2x10 are still flush. If the lath is in the right place, finish hammering the nail into the 2x10.

6. Double-check that your lath is on the line, and drive a nail into the other end of the lath, 3" from the edge.

7. Measure 6" from the lath you just installed, mark a crow's foot, draw a line, and repeat steps 4 through 6 with your next piece of lath. Repeat these steps over and over until you have lath every 6" along the whole length of the 2x10.

8. If your lath is longer than the width of the 2x10, use your handsaw to saw off the extra wood, so the pieces of lath are nice and even on both sides of the 2x10. Tip: Begin by placing the saw on your mark and pulling toward you. Lift the saw up and repeat until you make a small mark or groove in the wood. Then begin the back-and-forth sawing motion.

9. Once completed, lean your ladder into the opening of the chicken coop, and screw the ladder into the wood of the coop with a drill or impact driver, making sure the screws are parallel to the ground to ensure a good connection. You most likely will want to screw the ladder into the face of the coop to allow the door to fully close.

10. Let your chickens in to have a good time!

ARIYA

AGE: 11
LOCATION: Metairie, Louisiana
WHERE ARIYA LEARNS: Electric Girls

> *If you have a fear, just believe you can do it.*

What are some things you want us to know about you?

I live with my mom and my two brothers. I have one older brother and one younger brother. I like to read and do projects on the computer. I want to learn how to engineer and learn how to use tools and soldering and things. I really like reading, and books have a lot of interesting stuff because there are all different types of books. I like reading books about people, and comic books. Blue and purple are my favorite colors. My favorite tool is the soldering gun.

What is the first thing you ever built?

The first thing I built was a little car, and it had, like, moving wheels I recycled from an old plastic car. I made it out of old wood, sticks, and cardboard. It had little round light-up balls, and I used those as headlights. I was nine when I made it.

How does building make you feel?

Building makes me feel like I can build mostly whatever I want, and have the courage to do most stuff. And feel positive.

Why do you build?

I build mostly because it's fun. I like getting to use different types of tools and explore different types of things I can use.

What advice do you have for other girls?

Never be afraid to do something. Never listen to what other people say if it's negative.

What's the first step in trying something new?

Believe that you can do it, mostly. If you have a fear, just believe you can do it.

Who do you look up to?

I look up to a lot of people. Like my parents and my friends and family members. Because they help me and I can help them with other things.

What are some other activities that make you feel courageous, strong, and bold?

I like climbing and rock climbing. It makes me feel free and excited. I go rock climbing with my stepmom and my brothers and my mom.

What are some ideas of things girls can build at home?

Probably building a small little house out of cardboard, wood, Popsicle sticks, or like a little birdhouse.

What project are you sharing with us?

Last year at Electric Girls camp I built a two-story hotel and it had a downstairs and a café. It was called Unicorn Hotel.

CALLIE

AGE: 8½
LOCATION: Brooklyn, New York
WHERE CALLIE LEARNS: In her lab in her apartment
and at Curious Jane summer camps

> *Don't be scared by a blowtorch.*
> *If you ever use it on a cold day, put gloves on.*

What are some things you want us to know about you?

I'm learning to play the piano. I'm awesome. I like drawing but I'm not very good. I don't want to be the first woman president because then I'll have to fix *so much*. I want to be a playwright because I get to make plays. But I guess I don't really want to be a playwright; I want to be someone in a play. I can sing really fast. I like to wear my glasses backward and upside down. I don't know why, I just do. I also want everyone to know I invented the tuna and potato chip sandwich. You take bread and then you take some tuna, however you make it. First you drain the water from it and then you add mayonnaise. Then you spread your tuna onto the bread. You take potato chips—on these sandwiches, I prefer kettle-cooked—and place them on the tuna, and then you *crunch*! It's so good.

What is the first thing you ever built?

I think the first thing I ever built was with my Legos. I made a double Lego bunk bed. Because my figures, they were sisters and I wanted them to have a bed together. Like the sister I've always wanted.

How does building make you feel?

Happy because I get to create.

Why do you build?

I build because it makes me happy. I build because I enjoy new things being created.

What advice do you have for other girls?

Don't be scared by a blow-torch. If you ever use it on a cold day, put gloves on. One thing about my project, if your solder thingie balls up, that's not good and you need to add another piece.

Don't crack under pressure. Because if you crack under pressure, you show that you're scared. Even though being scared is good, you don't want to be scared all the time. Sometimes you have to be brave. What I do when I'm scared, I breathe.

Don't wear too much pink. Unless you choose to. Because if you wear too much pink, the boys will think you are dainty. And you're not dainty, you are *tough*. One time, there was a time to do something messy and all the girls said they wanted to do it and the boys didn't want to do it. Which proves girls like taking risks, and *they* should be the heroes in most books.

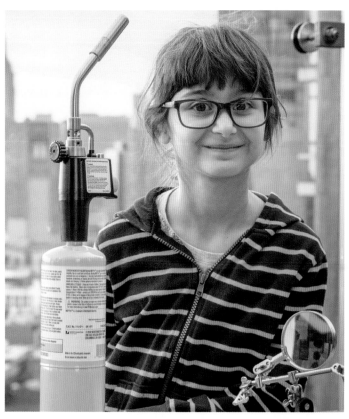

What's the first step in trying something new?

The first step in trying something new is making sure you're comfortable. Say, like, you're not comfortable using a Sharpie. You should *try* to get over it. But if you can't or you're still uncomfortable, don't do it. It's like stepping out of your comfort zone but not going too far that you can't find your way back in.

Who do you look up to?

I look up to Ruth Bader Ginsburg because she's basically an older version of me. She's Jewish, so am I. She's a girl, so am I. And she's left-handed, so am I. She did a lot of great things for the world, so that's another reason I look up to her.

I also look up to my mom because she's awesome. Because she's the one who taught me who I am. She's the one that taught me that girls don't have to be dainty. She's the one that helped me step *out* of my comfort zone.

What are some other activities that make you feel courageous, strong, and bold?

Doing tae kwon do. Because it has a lot of yelling involved. Because you're learning how to defend yourself, and every time there's a belt test, you can have something to feel proud about. It makes me feel bold and strong because even though people think it looks hard, it's not. You learn the basics and then you can do extraordinary things.

What are some ideas of things girls can build at home?

You can build Popsicle-stick houses and people. You can perhaps make robots. You can do anything at home as long as it doesn't involve too much fire.

What project are you sharing with us?

I made something called a "less angry owl." His name is Crackle. And he has another owl named Friend.

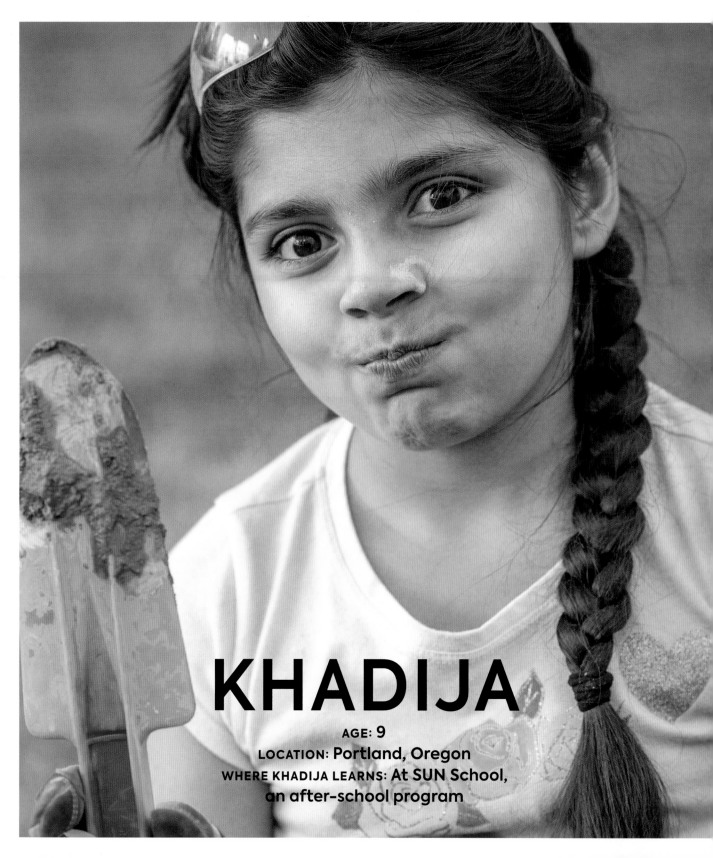

KHADIJA

AGE: 9

LOCATION: Portland, Oregon

WHERE KHADIJA LEARNS: At SUN School, an after-school program

> *Girls can have freedom. They don't have to stay at home or anything. They don't need to stay inside and do all the work. They can go and have some fun.*

What are some things you want us to know about you?

I don't really like pink that much. My favorite color is twilight. I like to do art and projects and stuff. I like all kinds of projects, including building things. I like to play lava monster or tag. I play a lot here at home with my friend Anfal. I live with my mom and dad and little brother and little sister. Well, actually I think I was born in Afghanistan. I speak English, Farsi, Hindu, a little Spanish, and Pashto. I like to plant stuff like flowers, and I like to spend time with my friends. My favorite thing to do in school is to write. I like writing stories using my imagination. Mostly about animals.

What is the first thing you ever built?

My first thing I ever built was a bridge out of Popsicle sticks. In school we were doing a project, and we were learning about bridges. We made one at school and we made one at home.

How does building make you feel?

It turned out great! I kind of felt excited. And proud.

Why do you build?

It is fun. When I made the planter box (see Project 2), putting in the powder was really cool. It was, like, floating.

What advice do you have for other girls?

Girls can have freedom. They don't have to stay at home or anything. They don't need to stay inside and do all the work. They can go and have some fun.

What's the first step in trying something new?

Just try it.

Who do you look up to?

I look up to my mom and dad because they help with hard stuff, and if I need it they give me advice. I look up to myself because I'm a really good person.

What are some other activities that make you feel courageous, strong, and bold?

I don't have to just be at my house with my mom and my sister while the boys are going out. I went to a park that had roller-coasters. I really wanted to go on the roller-coaster. I was so scared before I did it, and I felt brave after I got off.

What are some ideas of things girls can build at home?

Pencil holders out of toilet paper rolls.

What project are you sharing with us?

The concrete planter. I guess it was good. I don't like the color. Next time I would make the color really dark blue or black.

KHADIJA'S CEMENT PLANTER BOX

Khadija made this planter in the courtyard of her apartment complex while about thirty kids ran around her trying to help. She was excited to color the cement, and she chose two colors that she loved. Although she had done some building at school, she had never worked with cement. She made this project while her best friend, Anfal, was working nearby on her candleholder (see Project 8). Inspired by Anfal's outfit, Khadija changed clothes while her cement was drying so she would be more dressed up for her final photo. Pretty adorable.

MATERIALS

This project is fairly creative. Khadija used a shoebox-sized plastic bin as a form for the planter and two smaller tubs as forms for the plant spaces. You could use yogurt containers for the plant spaces, or anything about that size. The exact sizes are up to you.

❏ 1 large container made of plastic or wood, in the shape of the planter you want, about 3" h x 12" l x 6" w

❏ 2 smaller tubs (or however many can fit in the larger container), 3" diameter

❏ Nonstick cooking spray

❏ Cement All

❏ Water

❏ Concrete dye, if you want it

❏ Plants for however many openings your planter has

TOOLS

❏ Bucket for mixing (about four times as big as your final project. A 5-gallon bucket will never do you wrong)

❏ 1 gallon of water for mixing and cleanup. You can use a hose, or you can pour some water into a separate bucket

❏ Small shovel or trowel

❏ 1-quart measuring bucket (in paint section of hardware store)

SKILLS

❏ Putting on a ventilating mask properly

❏ Mixing cement

Adult oversight:

Cost after tools:

Safety gear:
• Safety glasses
• Cement-specific dust mask
• Vinyl (or nonvinyl) snug-fitting gloves

Work surface:
Pick a spot outside that you like—on the ground, in the grass—wherever you have space.

Skill level:

Time:

Dry time

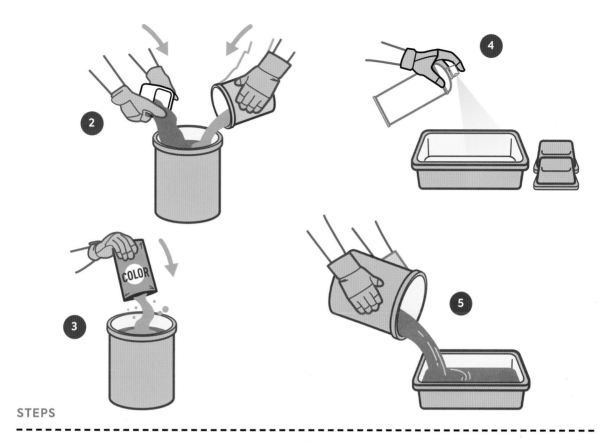

STEPS

1. Put on safety glasses and gloves. Check for and remove loose clothing and jewelry, and make sure hair is tied back.

2. To mix the cement, begin with about ½ quart cold water and add 2 quarts Cement All. Your consistency should be like a milkshake— thick enough that if you dragged the edge of your trowel through it, the line would remain for a few seconds.

3. If using dye, add it to the Cement All, and mix it in with a trowel. For two colors, first pour half the cement into another container. Khadija used a powdered dye, but you can use a liquid one.

4. Spray down the inside of your large container and the outsides of your smaller containers with cooking spray.

5. Pour the cement into the large container, filling it almost full, but leaving about 2" of room at the top. Note that Khadija mixed her cement in two rounds and poured two layers so her planter would have a layered look. We mixed on a hot day, and Khadija had to hurry during her second round of mixing so the first layer wouldn't dry completely.

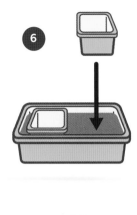

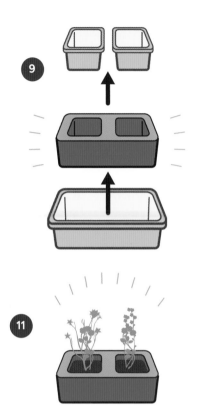

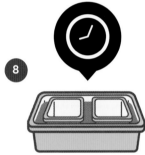

6. Fill your smaller containers about ¾ full with water. Carefully push them into the Cement All, going almost to the bottom. The water will help weigh down your space holder and keep them low in the cement.

7. Using the back of your trowel, gently pat the top of the cement. You can also use a slight jiggling motion. Move the trowel around the top of the cement, tapping and jiggling, so the cement will settle and have a flatter and smoother finish when dry. If space is tight, you can jiggle the entire container a little bit and try to smooth out any bumps.

8. Let everything sit for an hour.

9. When the Cement All feels solid (like a sidewalk), remove the smaller containers, by twisting gently and pulling up.

10. Turn the large container over gently onto a flat surface, and let the planter slide out.

11. Plant your plants. Khadija planted succulents, which require less upkeep. Place your planter wherever you will enjoy it most!

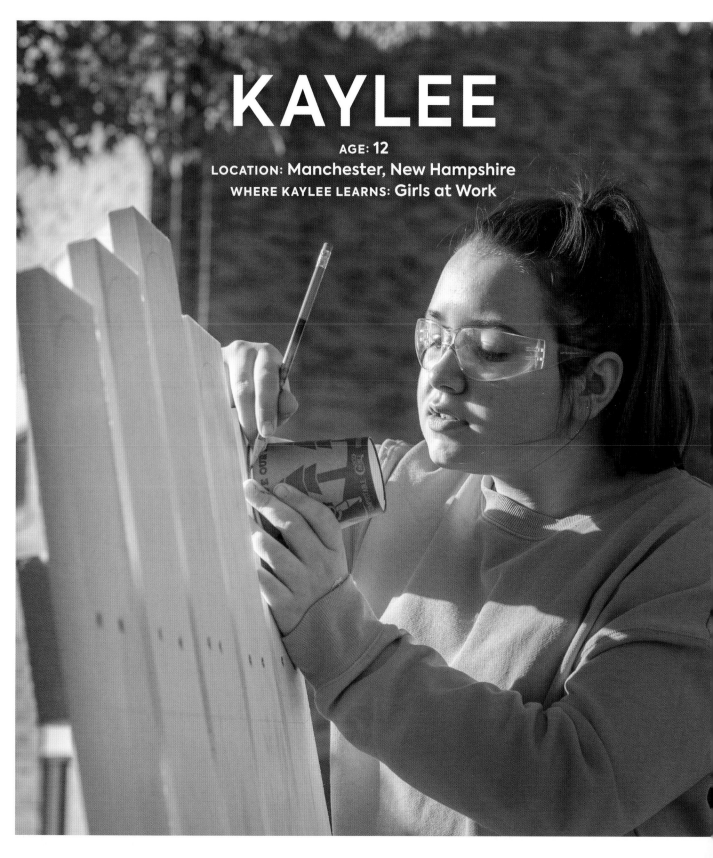

KAYLEE

AGE: **12**
LOCATION: **Manchester, New Hampshire**
WHERE KAYLEE LEARNS: **Girls at Work**

> ❝ *[Building] is fun and it makes me feel powerful.* ❞

What are some things you want us to know about you?
I like the color yellow. I love music through singing. I play basketball, soccer, and baseball.

What is the first thing you ever built?
My first project was a stool at Girls at Work.

How does building make you feel?
Building makes me feel strong.

Why do you build?
Because it is fun and it makes me feel powerful.

What advice do you have for other girls?
You can do anything. Don't let anyone tell you that you can't!

What's the first step in trying something new?
You just have to go for it and do it.

Who do you look up to ?
I look up to my mom because she is very independent and strong and also has a plan for anything that goes wrong.

What are some other activities that make you feel courageous, strong, and bold?
Chorus, basketball, and anything that someone doubts I can do.

What are some ideas of things girls can build at home?
Little boxes. You can fix things around the house.

What project are you sharing with us?
An Adirondack chair.

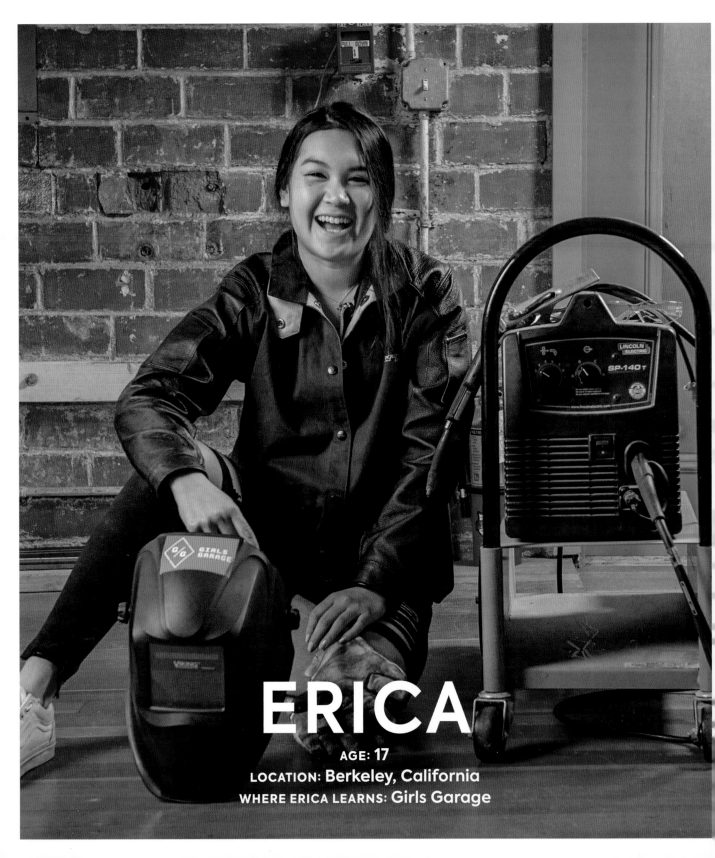

ERICA

AGE: 17
LOCATION: Berkeley, California
WHERE ERICA LEARNS: Girls Garage

> *Being able to adapt and listen to others is essential for building.*

What are some things you want us to know about you?

I am constantly working to be my best self in school and in life, with a growth mindset. I'm an extroverted optimist and seek positivity in my life! I feel I have to try new things in order to grow. As high school students, we have impossible standards to meet. We are expected to handle huge work loads, standardized test preparation, college applications, internships or jobs, and planning for our future. It can get really overwhelming! Consequently, I have been exploring the balance of academics, mental health, and all of the above. I love the arts and music. I played the violin for six years, danced for eight years, and played volleyball for four years. I love to cook and bake. I like art, from photography to designing/building to sketching.

I care a lot about my friends, family, and all things in general. I love hiking, traveling, and adventuring.

What is the first thing you ever built?

I believe the first thing I built was in fact a Popsicle-stick house! Me and my dad wanted to build a birdhouse to attract the birds that fly by his porch in Oakland, California—at this time I was super young, probably three or four years old. I remember eating a Popsicle almost every day, and waiting until we had enough to make the birdhouse. When we finally collected enough sticks, we sat down and glued each stick one by one, and bonded over that experience! The birdhouse lasted a very long time because it was covered by an overhead porch, and we watched the bluebirds stop by for a snack every day.

Additionally, my grandfather was an architect, carpenter, and so much more. As a result, he had been teaching me to understand how things work and how to fix things around the house since I was born. I learned how to use power tools at a young age, and how to problem-solve.

How does building make you feel?

Building and design are my creative outlets. They allow my crazy ideas and designs to become real. They give me a sense of satisfaction and accomplishment, a feeling that is so easy to become addicted to! Building brings immediate satisfaction, because with each step you are completing the project in front of your very eyes, much like photography or baking.

Why do you build?

The feeling of stepping back and looking at something that I built on my own (using extremely badass tools like chop saws and table saws) empowers me and reminds me that I am capable of these amazing things, just like all other girls are!

What advice do you have for other girls?

Insecurities are one of the biggest issues holding everyone back, and being afraid of failure. Everyone finds their confidence at different points in their life. You may be confident when you're cooking, or doing art in your room, but you may feel shy at school or when trying something new. My advice is to find something that makes *you* feel confident. Something that you love, like art, or talking to your friends, or reading, or video games, or anything! It is a great way to gain confidence in yourself, and to have something to do or a place to go if you get overwhelmed and need to come back to yourself. Knowing that you'll always have an activity you love, something you can come back to, allows you to create a safe space around yourself to escape the stress and take a break.

What's the first step in trying something new?

I believe the first step all people have to take is to mentally believe that you *can* do this new thing; you can start the process and *will finish it*, meeting your own standards to satisfy yourself along the way and feeling like you can overcome any obstacle you may face. You need to have the mindset that you *can* do it and *will* address any issues, without considering giving up. On the other hand, with building specifically, roadblocks could cause the whole project to go in another direction, and if this happens you have to have the mindset

that you can make the best of this setback—you have to believe that the end product will be great. A progressive mindset is really important to have. Being able to adapt and listen to others is essential for building.

It took me until high school to realize that I had to take a leap into trying new things if I wanted to improve myself, because there is no way to become a better version of yourself than to broaden your horizons and become more knowledgeable about the possibilities. *I can, I will, and I did.*

Who do you look up to?

I look up to individuals who use their power for the greater good, or make a positive difference in people's lives. There are so many people who are living with unfortunate circumstances, and so many who have the ability to make those situations better. I look up to these individuals because I've always wanted to make a difference that can change people's lives, but I haven't found exactly how I want to make my mark yet! Following these people on social media gives me daily inspiration to continue my journey and figure out who I am, or what I want to be. They give me hope, and remind me that there are other people who care and want to make a difference, like me.

Further, I look up to all people who are leaders and constantly uplift people in general to make a positive impact. I aspire to be a person that can make the best out of a bad situation.

What are some other activities that make you feel courageous, strong, and bold?

Being adventurous, swimming in the open ocean, jumping off cliffs into the ocean, snorkeling, hiking anywhere, finishing my homework on time.

The feeling of working with people older than me or more experienced, and surprising them with my skills! Learning from people and being able to grow from the experience makes me feel strong.

Talking to my friends and being able to open up to them, helping people get through their problems, teaching someone something, speaking up and out about my opinions, public speaking, trying something new and loving it.

What are some ideas of things girls can build at home?

A jewelry box, photo frame collage, gumball machine, planter box, or candleholder.

What project are you sharing with us?

A welded table I made at Girls Garage with a wooden tabletop, laser etched with a trolly.

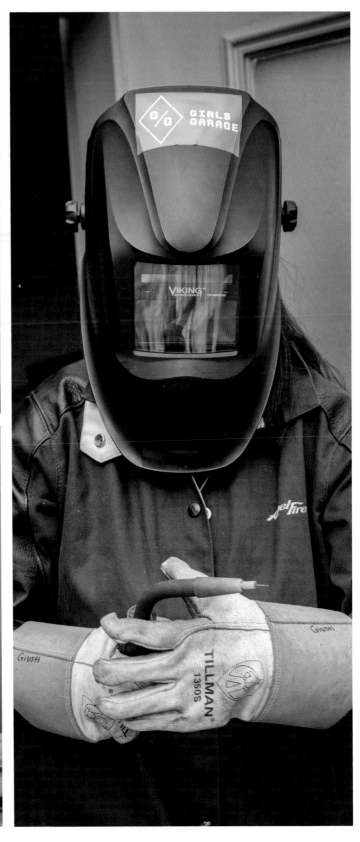

ATTALIA

AGE: 11
LOCATION: Grants Pass, Oregon
WHERE ATTALIA LEARNS: At home with her mom and at Girls Build

Keep trying and never give up. . . . When you try something new, make sure you feel happy when you're doing it.

What are some things you want us to know about you?

My favorite color is teal. I like drawing and reading. I've been doing Girls Build for three years now. I have three brothers and four cats.

What is the first thing you ever built?

The first thing I ever built was a leprechaun house. In first grade we were supposed to make leprechaun houses out of whatever we wanted. So I made a Lego leprechaun house.

How does building make you feel?

I like building a lot. It makes me feel really calm and happy. I really like using the chop saw and the drills, along with the other stuff when I get to build.

Why do you build?

I build because I like getting creative when I get to build stuff. And also when I get to use cool tools.

What advice do you have for other girls?

I would say to have fun when you're building. And pay attention to the instructors or coaches. Have fun when you try something new. Also, keep trying and never give up. Last, when you try something new, make sure you feel happy when you're doing it.

Who do you look up to?

I really look up to [bodybuilder] Ashley Nocera. She's really strong and funny. She's been my role model for a long time. Another one is [athlete] Demi Bagby. She's also funny and strong. They both have been really huge role models in my life.

What are some other activities that make you feel courageous, strong, and bold?

I like rock climbing a lot. I feel pretty strong when I do rock climbing. Also when I do skateboarding. I feel pretty good when I skateboard.

What are some ideas of things girls can build at home?

I think some ideas are like a Popsicle-stick house. Or pick up pieces of scrap wood and grab some nails, then see what you can create.

What project are you sharing with us?

The project I made was cement tea light candle holders. I made about half of them a reddish, orangish color. And the other half were gray. They were pretty fun to make.

ATTALIA'S
TEA LIGHT HOLDERS

Attalia headed to the river after dance class on a Friday night. Although the weather was typically hot that time of year, on that evening, rain threatened for much of the night. Eventually it began to pour. Attalia found a nice sandy part of the riverbank and got to work digging holes. The rain didn't stop her. Things got a little Zen as she kicked off her shoes and worked in the sand. The results were eight fun outdoor tea light holders that she placed on the path leading up to her home.

MATERIALS

❑ Sand. If you do not have a natural area for sand, you can use a large (24" x 24") cardboard box, or something similar. You'll need about 6" of sand (if you are buying it, that's a 50-pound bag).

❑ 1 box or bag of Cement All

❑ Cold water—about 1 gallon will do the trick

❑ Concrete color, if desired (see Materials Glossary)

❑ Cooking spray

Note: These tea light holders tend to be chunky and great for outdoor use.

TOOLS

❑ 1 trowel or small shovel for mixing

❑ 1 bucket or other container

❑ 8 tea light space holders—anything the size of a tea light and at least 2" deep (Attalia used glass tea light holders, but you can use any small container, as long as it's the right size—a minimum of 1½" diameter)

❑ One 1-quart bucket (available in the paint section of the hardware store)

SKILLS

❑ Cement mixing

❑ Digging

❑ A little artistic flair

Adult oversight:

Cost after tools:

Safety gear:
• Safety glasses
• Cement-specific dust mask
• Latex or nonlatex gloves

Work surface: Flexible

Skill level:

Time:

Dry time

STEPS

1. Put on safety glasses and gloves. Check for and remove loose clothing and jewelry, and make sure hair is tied back.

2. Begin by digging eight holes in the sand in any shapes you are excited about. If using store-bought sand, you will need to wet it. Attalia created circles and ovals, but you can do any shape you want. Remember to make them big enough to fit the tea light space holder, leaving ¾" to 1" of room around the edges and bottom of the tea light (dig holes at least 3" deep).

3. Make sure the bottom of each hole is fairly flat so the holders can sit on a flat surface once

they come out of the sand. Attalia also took a minute to measure her holes to make sure they were the right size and depth.

4. Put on your gloves and mask. Cement can burn your skin, so take your safety seriously. Read steps 5–10 before you start mixing, so you know what you are supposed to do and can work quickly.

5. Open the bag of Cement All. Set your mixing container next to it, along with a small bucket of water. Note: If you are doing more than one color, you need to mix multiple small batches instead of one big batch, because the cement will dry before you have a chance to pour.

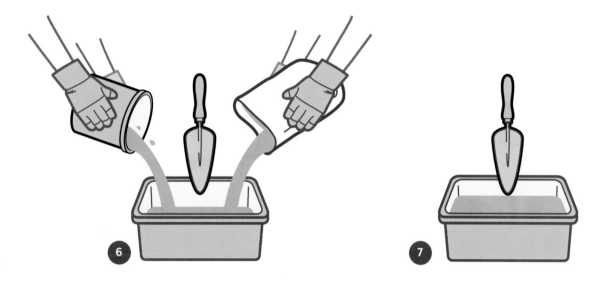

6. To make eight tea light holders with only one added color, use 3 quarts Cement All. Pour the Cement All into your mixing container. Even though you are wearing a mask, take care to pour close to your bucket to minimize dust. Add ¾ quart water to the Cement All, and begin mixing with a trowel or small shovel. As you stir, check for lumps in the mixture, and make sure to break them up with your trowel.

7. The final consistency should be like a milk-shake. If yours is too wet, add small amounts of Cement All until it is thick enough. If it is too thick or dry, add small amounts of water. Beware: When mixing concrete or cement, a little water goes a long way. If your mixture is dry, add no more than ¼ cup water. Mix and repeat until you get the right consistency.

8. If you want your tea light holders to be half gray and half colored, you need to pour the gray ones first, then color the remaining cement, then pour the remaining holders. Note: If you want a variety of colors, set out multiple containers to mix your colors in.

In the next step, pour your colors into these separate containers.

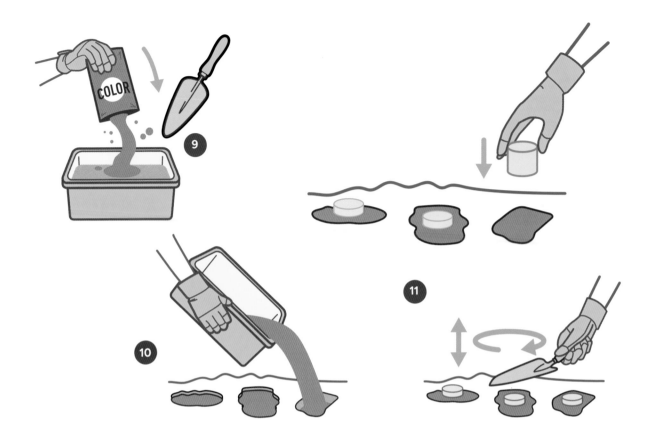

9. Coloring: If you want colored holders, add color to your cement until it is the shade you want. Attalia added a lot of color to get a nice dark red. If you want gray and one more color like Attalia did, mix and pour the Cement All first without adding color. Pour the number of holders you want to keep gray, then add color to the rest of the cement. Mix the cement very vigorously so the color is even throughout. Pour the colored cement into your remaining holes.

10. Pouring: Fill the holes you made in the sand with the Cement All mixture almost to the top, stopping about ¾" below the surface. Next, spray the outside of the space holders with cooking spray, then push them gently into the center of each glob of Cement All mixture, forcing each one down about 1".

11. Using the back of your trowel, pat the top of the Cement All around the space holder. Feel free to wiggle and jiggle it a little bit. This movement settles the Cement All and will make for a nicer

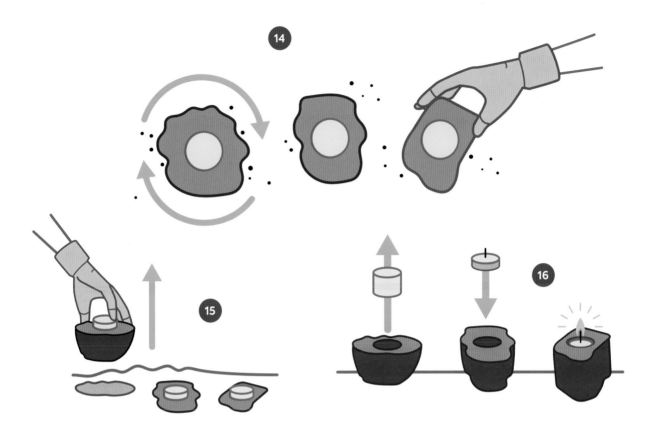

finished project. Tip: Tap the surface of cement anytime you pour it too (remember, this is cement, which is different). It settles the rocks away from the surface of the cement and makes for a nice, smooth finish.

12. Repeat steps 6 to 11 on any remaining holes.

13. You have one hour until your holders are ready. Time to clean up! Remember that cement can burn your skin, so wash up thoroughly using soap.

14. Once the cement is firm, after about an hour, you can take the space holders out by twisting them side to side, then pulling up and out. Do not attempt this step if the Cement All is still soft to the touch.

15. Dig your pieces out of the sand. Attalia brushed them off so the sand wouldn't stick.

16. Set your new holders out where you want them, and add real or electric tea lights. Your mood has been set!

AZI

AGE: 9
LOCATION: Portland, Oregon
WHERE AZI LEARNS: Girls Build

> *Building doesn't have to be perfect, but it's always inspiring. You can always do it over or change something as you go.*

What are some things you want us to know about you?

My favorite color is turquoise. I enjoy building, drawing, and doing origami. I like going to the library and reading mystery stories and graphic novels.

What is the first thing you ever built?

In kindergarten I built a bunch of fairy houses out of tree wood, sticks, bark, moss, leaves, seeds, and other things in nature.

How does building make you feel?

Building makes me feel encouraged, inspired, and happy!

Why do you build?

I build things because it makes me feel happy, and building things encourages me to build more.

What advice do you have for other girls?

Building doesn't have to be perfect, but it's always inspiring. You can always do it over or change something as you go.

What's the first step in starting something new?

The first step is thinking about materials and knowing that building something doesn't have to involve wood or just one thing. Something could be built out of many different things, like clay or paint or metal or wood or scraps.

Who do you look up to?

I look up to sculptors, and my mom and my grandma.

What are some other activities that make you feel courageous, bold, and strong?

In third grade I transferred to a new school, and I didn't know anybody. Now I do know them, and I feel courageous when I think about that.

What are some ideas of things girls can build at home?

A tree house or a dollhouse or a small box to hold special treasures.

What project are you sharing with us?

A sheet metal lamp, a concrete planter, and a coat rack.

MARILIE

AGE: 18
LOCATION: Colorado Springs, Colorado
WHERE MARILIE LEARNS: The MiLL

> *The one [piece of] advice that I always live up to is always pay attention. I use it at the MiLL so I don't cut my fingers, or mess up a machine or my project.*

What are some things you want us to know about you?

When I first started going to the MiLL I liked it a lot, and I began to think I could use these skills in a career. My first plan was to do singing, but the more I learned to like carpentry, I thought maybe I could sing as a hobby. I've been singing since third or fourth grade. I took choir and I began to like singing a lot, especially R&B. I live with my mom and dad, two younger sisters, and one younger brother—I'm the oldest. I like being the oldest sometimes, but other times it's hard to be in charge of them when they don't listen. But no matter what, I always have their backs. After I graduate I am planning on an internship at Concepts in Millwork; then I'll go to Red Rocks Community College to get my certificates. While I do that I'll be working at Walmart, and I'll live with my parents. I also do knife-skills competitions. In a knife-skills competition I'll be wearing a chef coat and chef pants, and my hair will be braided. There will be four people in the kitchen. They'll tell us to make four specific knife cuts, and we have to finish them before thirty-five minutes. There has to be 4 ounces of each ingredient that we cut. I don't want to be a chef, but I love to cook, and my teacher came up to me and was like, you should do this competition. This is my first year competing.

What is the first thing you ever built?

Okay, well, the first thing I ever built was this cabinet, but that was last semester. It turned out all right. There are some things I could have done better. We played Legos—sometimes we went by the book, but sometimes we would just let our minds go. It was actually pretty fun. We would make castles and houses.

How does building make you feel?

It's relaxing. It gets your mind off of things that stress or worry you. It just takes your mind off of everything.

Why do you build?

I just wanted to try it. I didn't think I would end up actually building things out of wood. I saw the machines and I was like, oh, I want to use those machines. I saw the table saw and the sanders. I've always wanted to sand—I don't know why. It's the machines that really got me. Right now my favorite machine is the miter saw. Last semester was the table saw.

What advice do you have for other girls?

I think girls should be able to do whatever they want to do. Nobody should bring them down. They should always know that they can do it, no matter what.

Who do you look up to?

I look up to my dad a lot. He gives us a lot of advice. Sometimes we listen and sometimes we don't. The one advice that I always live up to is always pay attention. I use it at the MiLL so I don't cut my fingers, or mess up a machine or my project.

What are some other activities that make you feel courageous, strong, and bold?

Swimming. I love to swim a lot. I like the competitive part, and the fact that it helps me work out and build my muscles. I also really love reading. If I was to choose my own project, I would make a bookshelf because I have a lot of books. I kinda get lost in the book. My favorite is the Divergent series, and I've read that many times. I read the Hunger Games series. I like that feeling where I can shut everybody out and just get into the book.

What are some ideas of things girls can build at home?

Well, I think an easy thing for little girls to build is probably a birdhouse or bookshelf. Or they could make little tables for when they play dress up. Or they could make something they are going to use, like little dressers or little picture frames.

What project are you sharing with us?

A table I made in class.

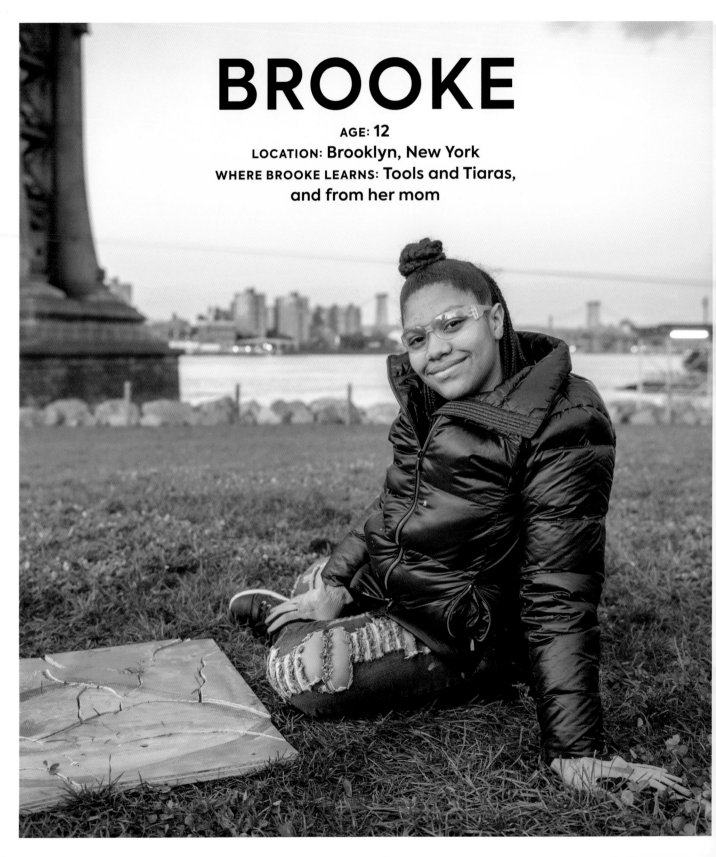

BROOKE

AGE: 12

LOCATION: Brooklyn, New York

WHERE BROOKE LEARNS: Tools and Tiaras,
and from her mom

> *The skills you learn [in building] are math, planning, problem-solving, organization, confidence.*

What are some things you want us to know about you?

I'm a twelve-year-old girl living in New York City, and am a seventh grader at Philippa Schuyler Middle School for the Gifted and Talented. I live with my parents, sister, and younger brother. I really like my school because it focuses on the arts as well as academics. One of the classes I am currently enrolled in is beginning steelpan [the steelpan is also known as the steel drum]. I like this class because, being West Indian, I think the pan is an extremely important instrument, and I am fascinated by the range of sounds you can create with it.

What is the first thing you ever built?

I helped my mother build a Native American cradleboard. It was a project for my fourth grade curriculum showcase. It is traditionally made out of wood, but I made mine out of sheet metal because my mother is a sheet metal worker and had access to all the materials I needed to replicate the cradleboard.

How does building make you feel?

Building makes me feel like I'm on top of the world. I like to build by myself just to accomplish what I can. Building is my hobby.

Why do you build?

I build to relax. I use many different tools and materials to build many different things. I also have the confidence to fix things that are slightly broken based on the skills I've learned from building.

What advice do you have for other girls?

I would tell girls to learn how to build so they can have the confidence to help themselves and be who they want to be. Building involves planning, which is also a good skill to have in life. Traditionally, building is looked at as a guy's job. But to me, building is just problem-solving. It's like looking at a puzzle and then putting it all together. Some puzzles have a ton of pieces, and some puzzles have a couple of pieces. The skills you learn are math, planning, problem-solving, organization, confidence. These are the only ones I can think of off the top of my head.

What's the first step in trying something new?

For me, the first step in trying something new is to wrap my mind around what it is I will be doing. Then I ask myself a bunch of questions like, Is it simple? Have I done this before? Will I have to use things I am unfamiliar with? Will I have to ask for help? I ask myself these questions to better understand what needs to be done, and I make a list of the things I am capable of and what I may need assistance with. If it's something that I have to do on my own, without any assistance, I will research it. Google is my best friend. I will read generally and then ask specific questions on Google about the things I still am not clear on. Reading and understanding how things work help me to build up my confidence in taking on new tasks. Once I feel confident, which is the most important thing for me, I just jump all in and get to work. Remember, even after taking all these steps it's still possible to mess up, and that's okay.

Who do you look up to?

I look up to the women in my house. I look up to my mother because she works as a sheet metal worker all day and still has time to make other projects. She just built her own bed frame. I look up to my sister because she is an EMT [emergency medical technician] for the fire department and responds to medical emergencies for the people of New York City. The women in my house are extremely hands-on and not afraid of challenges.

What are some other activities that make you feel courageous, strong, and bold?

When I was in my choir group that made me feel bold. It makes me feel bold because I had to perform in front of people. I would get a rush of adrenaline before I went on stage. I love to sing.

What are some ideas of things girls can build at home?

I would recommend starting off small. You can build whatever you want as long as you start small and work your way up. You could build, like, a house or a boat made out of Popsicle sticks. Then you can work your way up, like building a kite, which involves more than one type of material.

What project are you sharing with us?

I made a jigsaw puzzle out of wood. I spray painted a wooden board, and I used a jigsaw to cut it into pieces; then I put it back together.

BROOKE'S JIGSAW PUZZLE

Brooke built her jigsaw puzzle in Brooklyn Bridge Park with her mom and brother nearby. Her mom may be one of the coolest people I've ever met. She works on high-rise buildings in New York City, repairing and installing sheet metal ducting. Brooke created her jigsaw puzzle using precut wood, a cordless jigsaw, and spray paint (including a little bit of glitter spray paint). She then put her puzzle together in the park with her brother, Dash.

MATERIALS

- ❑ 1 piece of ¾" plywood, measuring 2' x 2' (you can purchase this size precut at most large lumber stores)
- ❑ Spray paint (we recommend about three colors)

TOOLS

- ❑ 2 pipe or bar clamps
- ❑ Jigsaw with rough or fine wood blade
- ❑ Optional: Pencil

SKILLS

- ❑ Clamping
- ❑ Using a jigsaw

Adult oversight:

Cost after tools:

Safety gear:
- Safety glasses
- Ventilating mask
- Gloves
- Ear protection

Work surface:
Workbench

Air space:
You will need an outdoor space or a well-ventilated indoor space to spray paint

Skill level:

Time:

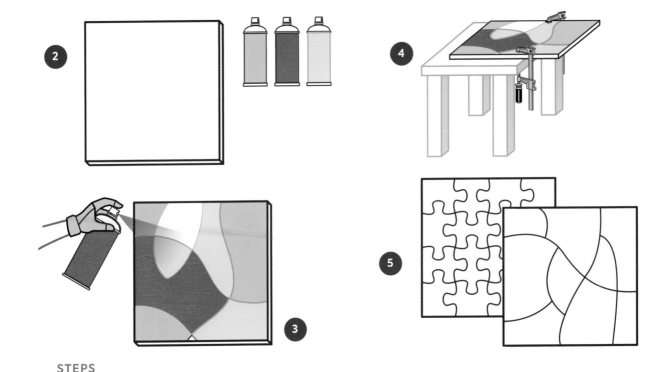

STEPS

1. Put on safety glasses, mask, and gloves. Check for and remove loose clothing and jewelry, and make sure hair is tied back. You should create this project outside or in a space where it is well ventilated.

2. It's time to get creative! Grab your spray paints, and begin painting your board in whatever way you feel inspired. Remember, if you paint the board and change your mind, you just need to let the first coat dry a little bit (about five minutes) before you paint over it. The great news is that you can paint it over and over again until you get just the look you are going for. The busier the better, as this will help make putting it back together more fun. Tip: If you have never spray-painted before, read the directions on the can.

3. Take off your mask and let the paint dry completely. Use your own judgment here, but know that your board shouldn't be sticky at all. It can take anywhere from thirty minutes to two hours, depending on the weather.

4. Turn your board over so the unpainted side is facing up. Clamp it to the workbench, leaving about ½ of the board on the table and ½ hanging over the edge. Make sure the clamps are very tight. Note: If your paint is not dry, it will get ruined in this step.

5. You can draw out your cuts, if you'd like. If you don't want to draw them, you can skip to step 6 and design as you go. Either way, you have two options for cutting your design. You

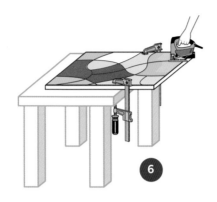

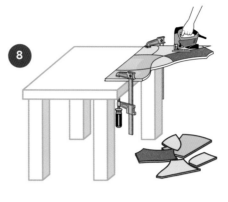

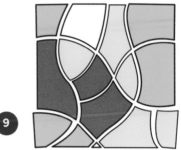

can cut it into the traditional jigsaw shapes that will hold together once the puzzle is put back together, or you can cut it into more of a mosaic, with pieces that slide together but don't interlock. If you choose to design at this stage, use a pencil, and draw out the lines you will cut. Or design it to look like Brooke's.

6. Now is the time to cut out your jigsaw puzzle. It's time to put on your ear protection. Place the table of your jigsaw on the board, with the blade away from the puzzle (the blade should not be touching wood when you start). Hit the trigger, and begin cutting slowly, either along your predrawn lines or on the path you choose as you go. Start by cutting the parts of the plywood that are hanging off the table.

Be aware of the table below your plywood. It is common to accidentally cut the table along with your board. Try to avoid doing this!

7. As you cut, let your cut pieces fall to the floor. They will be okay.

8. Once you have cut the pieces from the part of the board that was hanging off the table, unclamp the board and turn it sideways on your work surface. Reclamp it to the table and cut the remaining pieces. Repeat as necessary.

9. You should now have a pile of painted plywood at your feet. Find a buddy and a flat surface, and get to work putting your jigsaw puzzle together!

CAROLYN

AGE: 13
LOCATION: Colorado Springs, Colorado
WHERE CAROLYN LEARNS: The Twine Lab

> *"You gotta be proud of who you are, proud of being a girl."*

What are some things you want us to know about you?

I play soccer and run track—the 400 meter, the 200, and the 100. I *love* dogs a lot; they're my favorite. I'm very environmentally conscious. Well, I try to only eat sustainably sourced palm oil, limit my plastic use, and reuse bags at the grocery store. I'm in seventh grade. I want to be a primatologist when I grow up. I have a younger sister. I like to ski. I want people to stop using single-use plastic!

What is the first thing you ever built?

I've been playing with these kits called littleBits, and I competed in a challenge. We were supposed to build something for a pet, so I made this contraption with a light sensor, and when my dog would go to it, a tennis ball would come out. It was really cool. That was my best one.

How does building make you feel?

Happy and then focused and very concentrated. I can't really do two things when I'm building—I gotta kind of tune into building. I like that.

Why do you build?

It's just something to do, like trying to expand my horizons away from sports while experimenting with other things.

What advice do you have for other girls?

Everything in our society is changing right now. Girls are getting more power. You gotta advocate for yourself. You can't let other people push you around—you gotta be proud of who you are, proud of being a girl.

What's the first step in trying something new?

You can't go into it being negative. You gotta think positively about it. And if it stinks, you gotta push through it. Or quit. I mean, if it's awful, if you hate it, you can't bear it, you really shouldn't give up, but if it's really that bad, then you gotta think, maybe I can try a different something.

Who do you look up to?

I look up to my mom and dad. And Jane Goodall. Because they look at life from a really positive angle. And Jane Goodall (the world's

most famous primatologist) is an activist, which is pretty awesome, and she does what I want to do.

What are some other activities that make you feel courageous, strong, and bold?

Track, soccer, and skiing. Soccer because you can get injured at any second, so doing it makes me feel courageous. And they all take a lot of muscle. What makes me feel bold would be track because it's an individual sport. You rely on yourself and no one else.

What are some ideas of things girls can build at home?

They can build anything they want to! It's kinda fun to recycle because you can take something like an old toilet paper tube and make it into . . . binoculars.

What project are you sharing with us?

I made a bookshelf that could also be a plant shelf, which is an automatic air purifier. I wanted to go a lot faster but you gotta be patient so you don't mess up. Don't let your mom do the measuring.

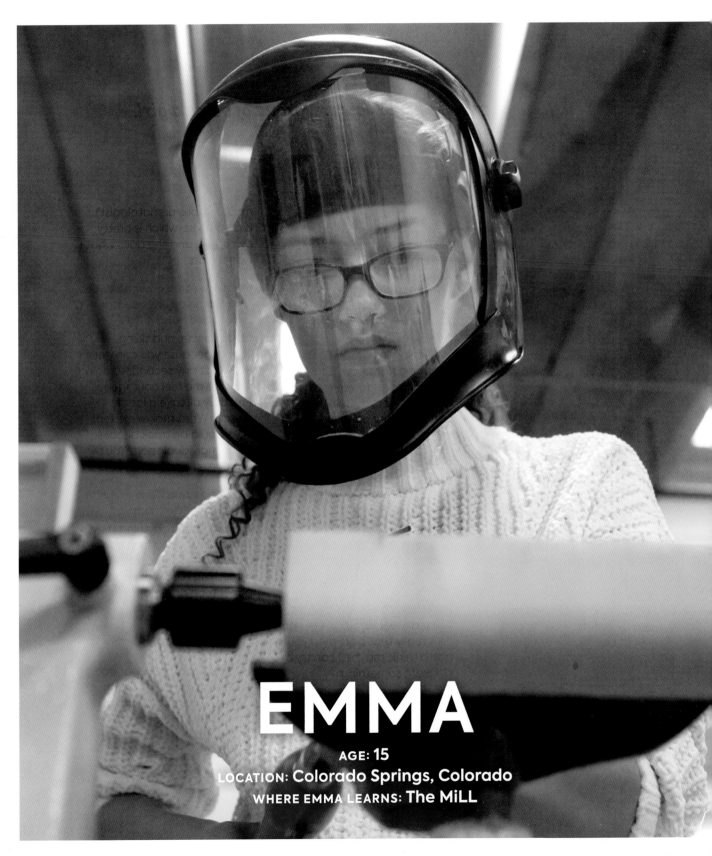

EMMA

AGE: 15
LOCATION: Colorado Springs, Colorado
WHERE EMMA LEARNS: The MiLL

> *I love to build things because I like the way you have to think if you want to create.*

What are some things you want us to know about you?

I have four sisters (one older, three younger) and a half brother and half sister. I am an aunt already. I play tennis after school, and when it's fall I play volleyball after school. My friend Giselle just taught me how to skateboard. I fell, which I knew would happen. It was kinda hard at first, but I taught myself to go down my driveway. I am pretty good at roller-skating, and it was kinda the same. Even though I'm pretty young, I'm into politics. Even though he's not very popular, I like Trump. I watch a lot of news. I do that a lot in my free time. My favorite tool is either the band saw or the lathe. You can do a lot on the band saw, but I like the lathe because it's relaxing and satisfying.

What is the first thing you ever built?

The first thing I built that I remember was when I was eleven, and it had significance to me. It was a paper air rocket and a CO_2 car, and they sparked more interest in STEM [science, technology, engineering, and math] programs for me. My middle school teacher Mr. Martinez helped me with it, so I thank him for that.

How does building make you feel?

Building makes me feel happy overall because I do have to focus and stuff, but I like to see how things work, and using the machinery is fun.

Why do you build?

I love to build things because I like the way you have to think if you want to create, and it's nice to keep the product of my work. It's nice to look at furniture and see how it's made, knowing more because I have built something using a similar process.

What advice do you have for other girls?

My advice for other girls and guys alike is to just do your personal best, find what you enjoy, and see if you can make a career out of it. My problem is I haven't narrowed down what my interests are.

What's the first step in trying something new?

Trying something new can be challenging, especially if there is competition, but when you're new, the best thing is to just absorb all the info you can so you can improve.

Who do you look up to?

I look up to Elon Musk because he's really smart and just invents and does whatever he wants.

What are some other activities that make you feel courageous, strong, and bold?

Some other activities are sports like tennis, volleyball, and roller-skating because I like to learn technique and improve myself.

What are some ideas of things girls can build at home?

People can build anything in their area of experience; just make sure to plan to avoid costly mistakes. Anything from jewelry boxes to tables.

What project are you sharing with us?

On the lathe, I made two pens: one for my mom on Mother's Day and another for my dad on Father's Day. I also made two handles on the lathe for my table (one is a spare for when the other gets warped).

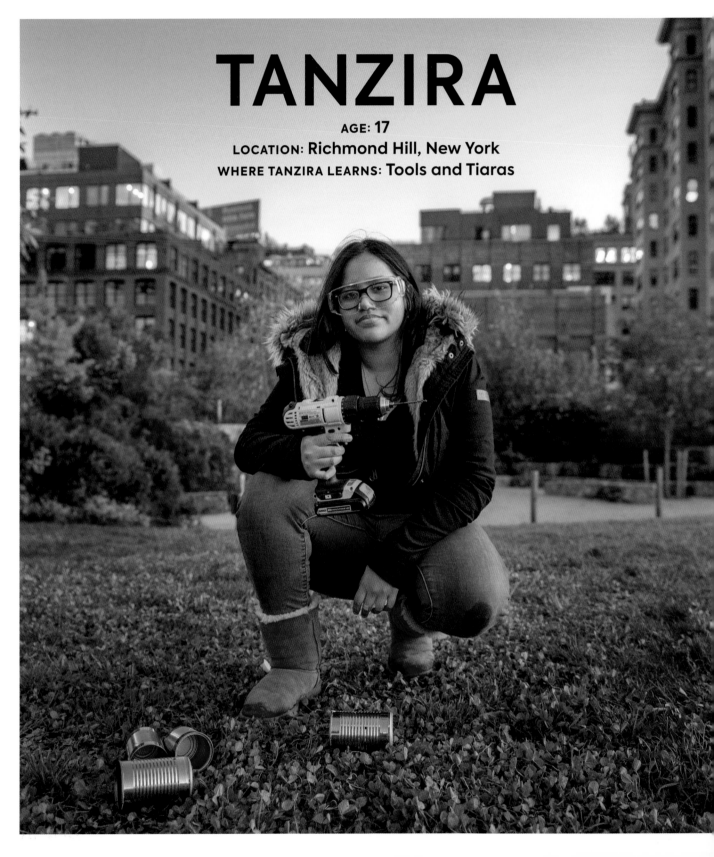

TANZIRA

AGE: 17

LOCATION: Richmond Hill, New York

WHERE TANZIRA LEARNS: Tools and Tiaras

> *Be strong. Be bold. Be fearless.*

What are some things you want us to know about you?

I come from a Bengali immigrant family. Being from such a culture, I was never exposed to the building industry growing up. The only acceptable career path in my parents' eyes was the medical field. I discovered what construction was when I got admitted into my high school, the High School for Construction Trades, Engineering, and Architecture. Here, I got exposed to the intricate craft and detail that go into building the structures around us. This was where I fell in love with construction. It amazed me that for the majority of my life I never knew who built houses and the buildings around me, and now I can't imagine myself in any field other than construction today.

What is the first thing you ever built?

The first thing I ever built was an Ikea stool. We were remodeling our home and bought multiple furniture pieces. Usually my brother would build the furniture we got; however, for some reason, he couldn't build this stool. I took a shot at it and in a matter of ten minutes I was done assembling it. I felt proud being able to build something my brother couldn't. To say my brother was shocked was an understatement.

How does building make you feel?

Building makes me feel empowered and strong. It makes me feel like the world is limitless. Being able to use power tools that many will never step close to gives me a sense of pride because I am working on something out of the ordinary. However,

with building comes blood, sweat, and tears, especially as a woman, and yet when you see the final product of what you created, no words can describe it. Building allows me to understand and appreciate the world around me.

Why do you build?

I build because it is intriguing to me how from just a piece of paper such amazing structures can be built. With the proper knowledge and bare hands, one can truly build anything. In addition I build because one day, I want to be able to walk the streets of different cities and see my work in the skyline, showing my loved ones how my creations have impacted the world for many years to come. I aspire to inspire future generations of women to be unafraid of breaking gender roles because there is no conventional job for a woman.

What advice do you have for other girls?

Advice that I have for other girls is to always remember your worth, no matter if it is in school, work, or your social life. Even though I've had experience in the workforce starting at a young age, many try to doubt my knowledge because of my gender, but they never ask about the experience I have in my major. Always stand your ground and show people the knowledge you have. Don't be afraid to stand out or challenge someone's way of thinking. Remember that you belong anywhere you go, and no one should say otherwise. Be strong. Be bold. Be fearless.

What's the first step in trying something new?

The first thing in trying something new is creating an open mindset and realizing that things may not go as planned. With any new activity comes a learning experience. Be willing to fail to succeed. No one is ever perfect in anything they start, but with practice, perfection will come. Also, you might end up falling in love with that new activity you tried, but you will never know unless you go for it.

Who do you look up to?

I look up to Judaline Casssidy. She was one of the very first women accepted into Plumbers Local 371, Staten Island, New York, and the first woman elected to the Examining Board of Plumbers Local No. 1. Judaline has inspired me to pursue a career in construction because I was originally hesitant to join a career that is male dominated and cutthroat. But it is something I truly love. After meeting her, I saw how she and many other women succeeded in this field because of their passion and drive for it. I found the motivation to pursue my passion because of her. With her nonprofit organization, Tools and Tiaras, she has taught me to be unapologetically fearless and authoritative while also teaching me the importance of sisterhood, because a support system can make the difference between being average or extraordinary. On days when it may be rough, I think about her and imagine how she didn't let anyone or anything get in her way of pursuing her dreams. I hope to inspire the future generation of females to break gender stereotypes, just like how she inspired me.

What are some other activities that make you feel courageous, strong, and bold?

Whenever I am in my school's carpentry shop and have my tool belt on and hammer in my hand, I feel as if I can conquer the world. Being able to say that at the age of seventeen I can build a house makes me feel bold. Not many people my age can say that. When I walk the beautiful streets of New York I am able to understand how the structures around me were built, and that makes me feel courageous because of how many people understand the environment around them. Whenever I tell someone I am in construction, I love seeing the shock on their face, because many people see it as a male's field. It is empowering to know that I am breaking gender stereotypes in the workforce, one step at a time.

What are some ideas of things girls can build at home?

A Popsicle-stick bridge or house, furniture, and jewelry boxes.

What project are you sharing with us?

Tea light luminaries.

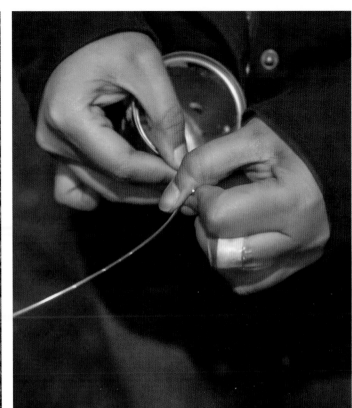
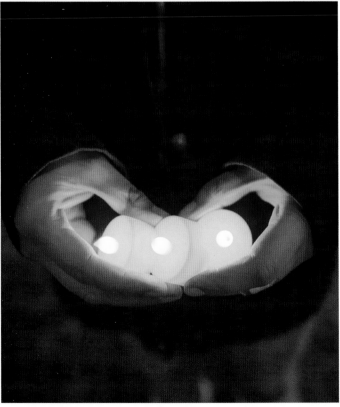

TANZIRA'S TEA LIGHT LUMINARIES

Tanzira showed up late for her photo shoot after the train she took from her SAT prep class got held up. Her dusk arrival was the perfect time to create these luminaries, and we were more than happy to hang out in the park as Tanzira got to work. This delightful teenager is driven and passionate about the trades, and she showed some real grit when working with the slippery cans! She worked on the grass without clamps because she is super skilled, but if this is your first time, you'll want a table and some clamps.

MATERIALS

❏ 3–5 clean tin cans, any size, empty and without lids and labels (it's best if the openings are not sharp)

❏ Wire (between 16 gauge and 20 gauge), about 12" per can

❏ Electric tea lights, 2 to 3 per can

> A note about wire gauge: Did you know that the higher the number, the smaller the wire? So 16-gauge wire is actually *thicker* than 20-gauge wire. Now you know!

TOOLS

❏ Permanent marker (optional)

❏ Pipe or bar clamps

❏ Drill

❏ Various sizes of drill bits, at least three that are dramatically different from each other

❏ Wire snips or wire cutters (your pliers may have a part that can cut wire)

❏ Pliers, either needle-nose or slip-joint

❏ Measuring tape

SKILLS

❏ Drilling

❏ Clamping

Adult oversight:

Cost after tools:

Safety gear:
• Leather or other cut-resistant gloves
• Safety glasses

Work surface:
Something clampable, like a work table

Skill level:

Time:

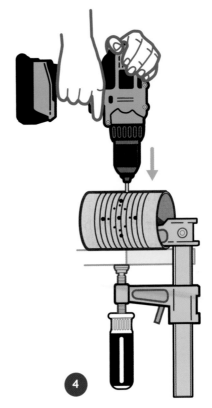

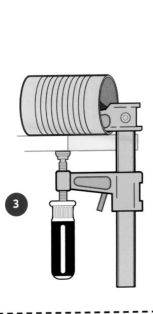

STEPS

1. Put on safety glasses and gloves. Keep gloves on at all times while holding the can. See page 36 for safety notes on gloves and drills. Check for and remove loose clothing and jewelry, and make sure hair is tied back.

2. You can design your cans by marking small holes on them with your Sharpie, or do as Tanzira did and be inspired as you drill. If using a Sharpie, you can draw a simple scene, draw a design, or place dots at random. Two things to remember: The more holes you drill, the more effective your luminary will be, and you have different-sized bits, so the holes can be different sizes.

3. Once you have decided on a design (even if that design is no design), place the can on its side on a work surface. Clamp it onto your work surface.

4. Now that the can is secure, you can begin drilling. The drill bit is going to want to slide, so press down with some effort, but hit the trigger lightly. Once the bit bites the metal, you can press the trigger harder. Be prepared—once the bit goes through the metal, it will drop quickly through the can. Just be ready! As needed, unclamp your can, rotate, and reclamp to complete your design.

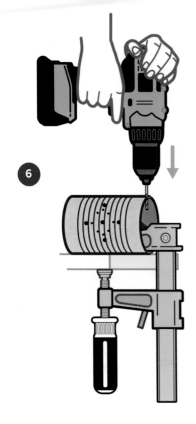

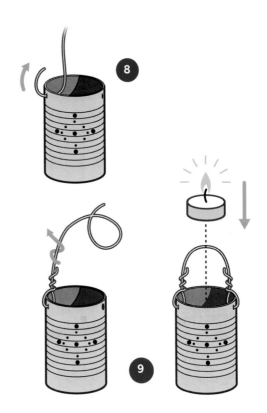

5. Repeat steps 3 and 4 on your remaining cans.

6. When you are done drilling all the holes you marked, it's time to drill the holes for your hanging wire. Mark a spot at least ¼″ below the top of each can. For this hole, use a bit at least as big as your wire. Once you make one hole, visually find a spot directly across the can, and make another hole there. These are the holes your wire will go through to suspend your luminary.

7. Making sure you are wearing your gloves, cut your wire to about 12″. It can be longer or shorter depending on the length of wire you want your lantern to hang from. If you use a 12″ wire, your luminary will hang about 4″ below the top of the wire loop.

8. Slide one end of the wire through one of the holes, pushing at least 2″ out through the can. You can use your fingers to make a loop and twist the wire around itself. If that doesn't work, you can use your pliers.

9. From the inside, slide the loose end of the wire through the opposite hole. Make a loop, and wrap the wire around itself.

10. Complete these steps on each of your cans, and you will have a luminary set, just like Tanzira. Drop in your tea lights and enjoy!

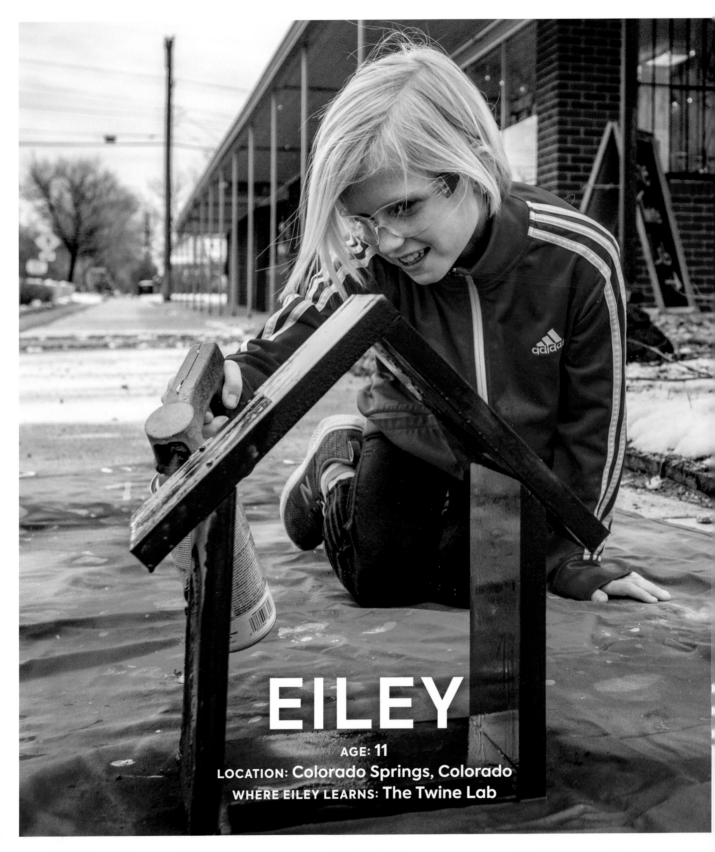

EILEY

AGE: 11

LOCATION: Colorado Springs, Colorado

WHERE EILEY LEARNS: The Twine Lab

> *You can build anything, and it doesn't have to be with nails and screws—you can build with nature and glue, or build a cake.*

What are some things you want us to know about you?
I play soccer and I am funny.

What is the first thing you ever built?
Probably a homemade rainbow loom with my dad.

How does building make you feel?
Free. Like nobody will judge me unless I want them to.

Why do you build?
Because it's fun to be creative. And building helps you build new relationships. I've made lots of new friends like Laney and Oliver at the Twine Lab.

What advice do you have for other girls?
You can build anything, and it doesn't have to be with nails and screws—you can build with nature and glue, or build a cake. Building comes in many different forms.

What's the first step in trying something new?
Picture it first.

Who do you look up to?
I don't really look up to anybody. I'm going on my own path.

What are some other activities that make you feel courageous, strong, and bold?
Playing soccer and field hockey—I just tried that and it's pretty cool. I also feel strong and creative when I put together fashionable outfits.

What are some ideas of things girls can build at home?
You can build cakes. You can build with nature, old toys, and recyclables. I used to make vending machines with old cereal boxes—we used our imagination.

What project are you sharing with us?
A bookshelf that I am giving to my grandparents for both their birthdays because they are near each other.

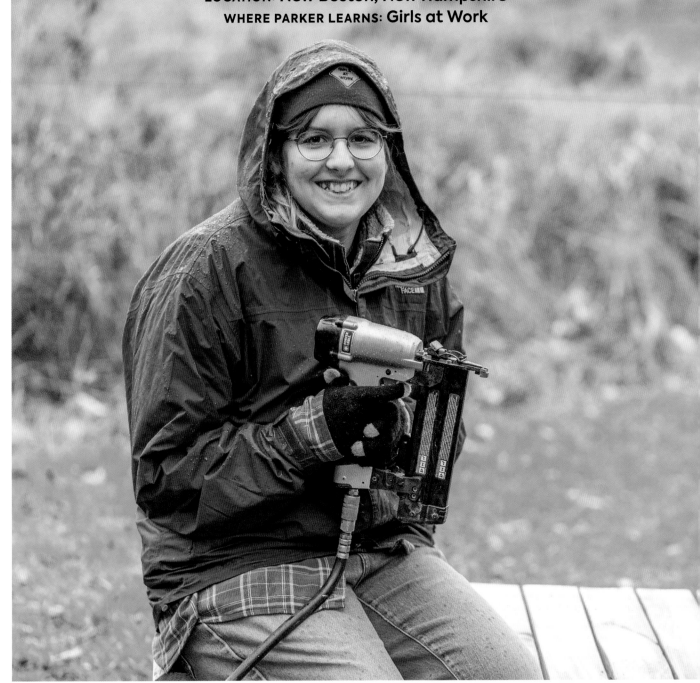

PARKER

AGE: **17**
LOCATION: **New Boston, New Hampshire**
WHERE PARKER LEARNS: **Girls at Work**

> *Building makes me feel strong,*
> *both mentally and physically.*

What are some things you want us to know about you?

I'm a math nerd and an anime and sci-fi geek. I also want to build theater sets as a career one day, since I enjoy it so much.

What is the first thing you ever built?

The first thing I ever built or helped build was a theater set for the Boys and Girls Club in Milford. I started it for community service hours for school but kept doing it after I got all my hours.

How does building make you feel?

Building makes me feel strong, both mentally and physically.

Why do you build?

I build because I like doing hands-on things. I also want to build as a career one day, and programs like this are good practice.

What advice do you have for other girls?

Ms. Elaine at Girls at Work is not that scary once you get to know her.

What's the first step in trying something new?

Ease into it and don't go all the way the first time, since that will make it more stressful to do new things.

Who do you look up to?

I look up to my dad, since he is very supportive of my career choice and is always giving new and very creative ideas. I also look up to Elaine, since she encourages me to do better and pushes me past my limit to make me stronger.

What are some other activities that make you feel courageous, strong, and bold?

Math, since I'm really good at it and it makes me feel smart when I know more or understand something before everyone else.

What are some ideas of things girls can build at home?

If you're just starting out, things like pegboards, small tables, and stools would be good to build for others or just to have at your home.

What project are you sharing with us?

A coffee table.

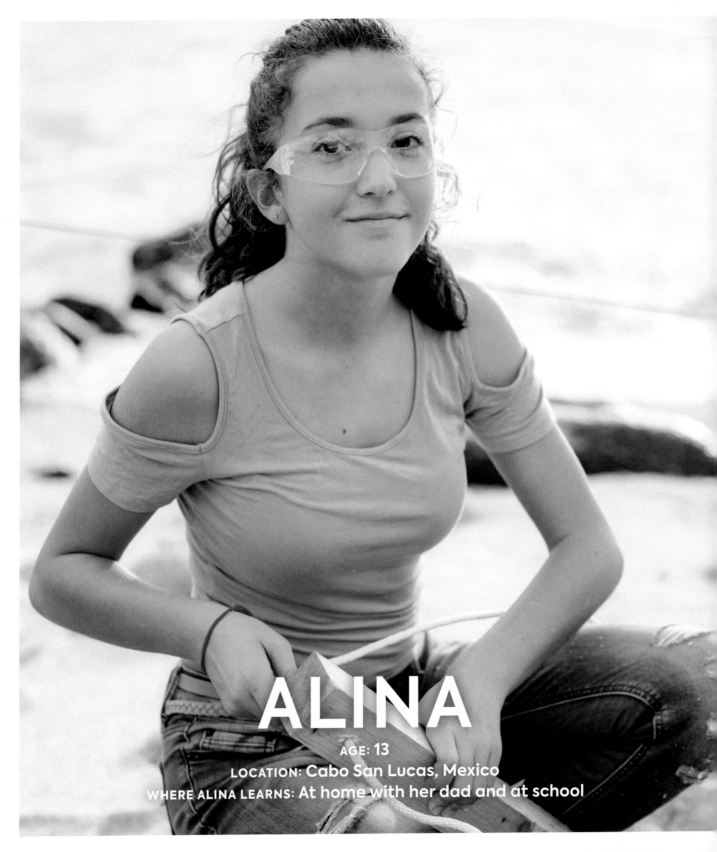

ALINA

AGE: 13
LOCATION: Cabo San Lucas, Mexico
WHERE ALINA LEARNS: At home with her dad and at school

> *I love decorating, and if I build it, it's more fun and less expensive at times.*

What are some things you want us to know about you?
I like to draw, paint, sing, and write music.

What is the first thing you ever built?
A big Lego spaceship with my cousins.

How does building make you feel?
Empowered.

Why do you build?
To create something and to be able to say you were part of it.

What advice do you have for other girls?
Do what your heart is set on.

What is the first step in trying something new?
Go in with a good attitude, because if you try something new but you are uninterested, then you might not like it as much as if you went in encouraged.

Who do you look up to?
My favorite singer, Billie Eilish, because she has been singing since she was such a young age and has gotten so far in only a couple of years, not to mention that she is very talented and kindhearted.

What are some other activities that make you feel courageous, strong, and bold?
I do boxing and MMA [mixed martial arts], and ever since I started I feel stronger and more in control.

What are some ideas of things girls can build at home?
Anything for your room! I love decorating, and if I build it, it's more fun and less expensive at times. It's a good activity.

What project are you sharing with us?
I made a wooden doormat.

ALINA'S WOODEN DOORMAT

Alina built her wooden doormat on a large, flat rock on the beach. Since most of the work involved tying knots, she used the rock as her building surface for both cutting and tying. Her dad, who she does projects with, stood nearby, watching proudly. A side note: Since most building in Mexico uses bricks and concrete, we had a hard time finding 2x2s. They are not common, and we had to have them custom ripped. Due to translation errors, the boards Alina used are actually 2″ x 2″, instead of 1½″ x 1½″, which is the standard size for a 2x2 in the United States. If the boards in the photos for this project look a little big, that's because they are!

MATERIALS
❏ Three 8' 2x2 cedar boards
❏ About 14' of ¼″ nylon rope

TOOLS
❏ Tape measure
❏ Pencil
❏ Speed square
❏ Jigsaw or chop saw
❏ Drill
❏ ⅜″ drill bit for wood
❏ Lighter (for adult use only)
❏ Heavy-duty scissors to cut the rope

SKILLS
❏ Measuring
❏ Drilling
❏ Sawing
❏ Knot tying

Adult oversight:

Cost after tools:

Safety gear:
• Safety glasses
• Ear protection
• Gloves (optional)

Work surface:
Flat table or workbench (or flat rock on the beach!)

Skill level:

Time:

STEPS

1. Put on safety glasses and ear protection. Check for and remove loose clothing and jewelry, and make sure hair is tied back.

2. Measure your 2x2s to 18", marking each measurement with a crow's foot and drawing a nice straight line with a speed square. Remember, the wide edge of the speed square hangs over the board and is held snugly against the edge. You will need 12 18" boards. If you are using 8' boards, you cannot measure the lengths in a row. Refer back to the section "Using a Tape Measure" (in "Skills") to see why.

3. Measure each 18" board one at a time, cutting after each measurement before measuring the next one. Cut each board. For this step, a chop saw will provide the cleanest

cuts, but Alina did a really nice job on hers using the jigsaw.

4. On one of your newly cut 18" boards, measure 2" from each end. Mark a crow's foot, then draw a line through the crow's foot with your speed square.

5. Repeat this on each of your 2x2s.

6. Once these lines are drawn, find the center of each line. To do this, you need to measure ¾" across the line, which means you'll need to burn an inch (see page 29). Find the ¾" mark, and mark a crow's foot.

7. Make sure your crow's foot is on your 2" line. You should now have two marks on each of your boards.

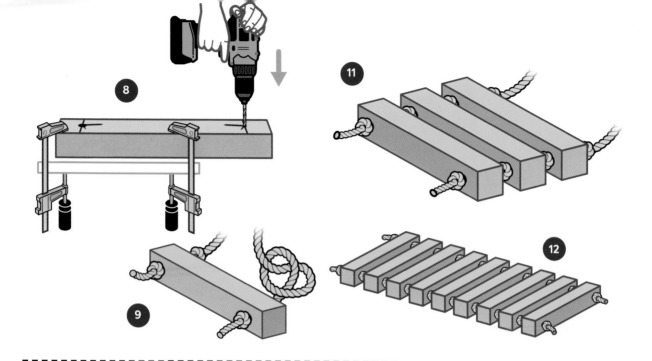

8. Place your bit in your drill. Clamp your wood onto a solid surface, leaving the marks overhanging, because you are going to drill all the way through. Using two hands, drill slowly into the wood, going straight through. Once you have run the bit through, go up and down (all the way through) a few more times to make sure the hole is clear. This will ease the path for your rope. Repeat this step on each of your boards.

9. Once all your holes are drilled, you are ready to run the ropes through them. First, cut the rope in half. Have an adult burn each end of the two rope pieces if they have not been burned already. Let an adult do this step. This will make it much easier to run the rope through the holes. Once both ends of both lengths of rope are burned, tie a knot in one end of each rope.

10. Take one rope and run the end that isn't knotted all the way through the first board. Tie a knot nice and tight against the board. Do the same with the other rope through the other end of the same board.

11. Slide the rope through the next board, then tie knots again. Repeat this with every board.

12. Once complete, tie your last knot very tight. Cut the remaining rope off, and have an adult burn the end. Your wooden doormat is complete!

ANGELINA

AGE: 11
LOCATION: Manchester, New Hampshire
WHERE ANGELINA LEARNS: Girls at Work

> *[Building makes me feel] happy.*
> *I feel like I'm in a good place and feel joyful.*

What are some things you want us to know about you?

I like drawing and playing sports (soccer, volleyball, basketball, swimming, track, and tennis). I play violin and clarinet in my school orchestra.

What is the first thing you ever built?

I built an Adirondack chair during my first class at Girls at Work.

How does building make you feel?

Happy. I feel like I'm in a good place and feel joyful.

Why do you build?

It helps make you not think about what is going on around you—at home, but especially at school, where there is bullying and fights.

What advice do you have for other girls?

This place—Girls at Work—will empower you more than your expectations.

What's the first step in trying something new?

Find something that isn't too challenging and isn't too easy. If you pick something too easy, what's the point? And if it's too hard you won't complete it. But if it is medium it will come out like you expected with a touch of something new.

Who do you look up to?

Heidi and Elaine at Girls at Work. Ms. Elaine helps me feel empowered and safe. Ms. Heidi because she makes me feel safe and comforts me when I need it.

What are some other activities that make you feel courageous, strong, and bold?

Orchestra because I get lost in the music and can play my heart out.

What are some ideas of things girls can build at home?

A treasure box, pegboards.

What project are you sharing with us?

I made a lap desk.

HARLEY

AGE: **13**

LOCATION: **Seaside, Oregon**

WHERE HARLEY LEARNS: **Girls Build summer camp**

> **[My mom] tells me I can do things,**
> **and she tells me I am strong and healthy.**

What are some things you want us to know about you?
I am different but the same, and I want people to love me. I swam in the Special Olympics this year and won two gold medals!

What is the first thing you ever built?
A gingerbread house for Christmas.

How does building make you feel?
Happy.

Why do you build?
Because it's fun.

What advice do you have for other girls?
Try new things.

What's the first step in trying something new?
Telling yourself you can do it!

Who do you look up to?
Mom because she helps me. She tells me I can do things, and she tells me I am strong and healthy.

What are some other activities that make you feel courageous, strong, and bold?
Dancing and bike riding.

What are some ideas of things girls can build at home?
A library, stool, planter, boxes, or shelf.

What project are you sharing with us?
Little Free Library.

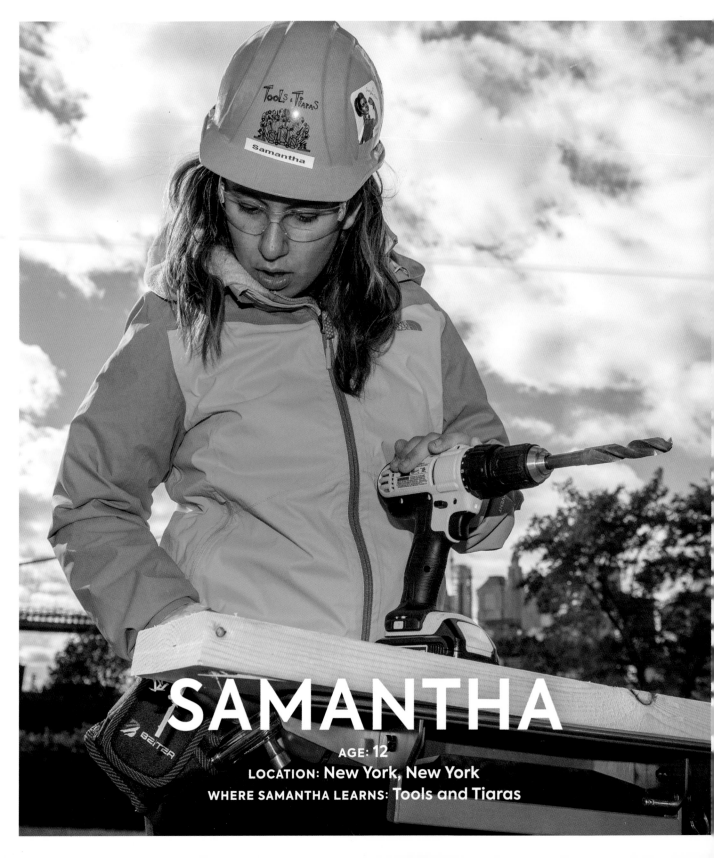

SAMANTHA

AGE: 12
LOCATION: New York, New York
WHERE SAMANTHA LEARNS: Tools and Tiaras

> *I like to build because it makes me feel like I am part of our world.*

What are some things you want us to know about you?

I am a Girl Scout Cadette. I love cats, adventure, and getting down in the dirt, and my favorite mythical creatures are dragons.

What is the first thing you ever built?

The first thing I built that I can remember is a miniature fortress made from wooden blocks, plastic cups, and jumbo-sized Popsicle sticks.

How does building make you feel?

Building makes me feel happy and joyous because I get the chance to turn something from a dream into reality.

Why do you build?

I like to build because it makes me feel like I am part of our world.

What advice do you have for other girls?

For other girls I give this advice because it helps me get through life: Get into many after-school programs, and get out there and explore the world around you. Find out *everything* you can.

What is the first step in trying something new?

Always prepare beforehand, and then you can dive into whatever you're planning!

Who do you look up to?

I look up to Judaline. She leads a girls' summer camp called Tools and Tiaras, which shows girls opportunities and careers that aren't stereotypical for women and girls. It empowers the girls that go to this camp.

What other activities make you feel courageous, strong, and bold?

I love to draw, zip-line, and swim, as well as rowing.

What are some ideas of things girls can build at home?

They can build with Legos, and can create anything that pops into their heads.

What project are you sharing with us?

A swing that can hang on a bar or a tree, and it is so much fun to swing on! I loved building it!

SAMANTHA'S SWING

Samantha built her swing in Brooklyn Bridge Park with tourists and locals humming about. Her mom spent the time warding off a park ranger who thought that Samantha's workbench was furniture and therefore shouldn't be allowed in the park. Although Samantha was serious while working, her demeanor completely changed when she finished her swing and put it to use. It's pretty fun to swing on a swing you built in Brooklyn Bridge Park.

MATERIALS

- ❏ At least 24" of 2x6 (see step 2)
- ❏ ½" braided nylon rope (or rope of a similarly strong material)

> How much rope do you need? Well, you'll need to know where your swing will hang. Measure that length, add 6', then double it. Rope = (Length + 6') x 2.

TOOLS

- ❏ Tape measure
- ❏ Pencil
- ❏ Speed square
- ❏ Lighter (for adult use only)
- ❏ Handsaw, chopsaw, or jigsaw
- ❏ Two bar clamps
- ❏ Drill
- ❏ ⅝" drill bit
- ❏ Heavy-duty scissors to cut rope

SKILLS

- ❏ Measuring
- ❏ Drilling
- ❏ Clamping

Adult oversight:

Cost after tools:

Safety gear:
- Safety glasses
- Gloves (optional)
- Ear protection

Work surface: Flat table

Skill level:

Time:

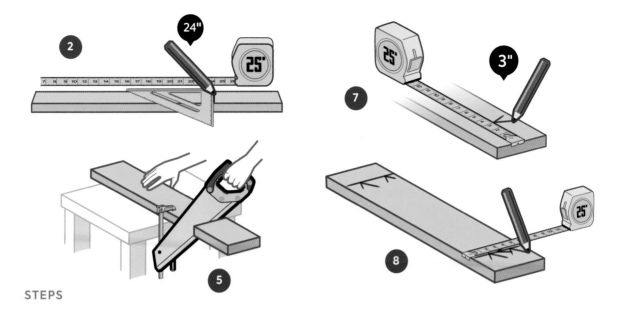

STEPS

1. Put on safety glasses and ear protection. Check for and remove loose clothing and jewelry, and make sure hair is tied back.

2. Mark your wood at 24". (This is actually a flexible measurement. Want a longer swing? Make this measurement longer. Make it shorter if you want a shorter swing.) Draw a crow's foot at 24" (or your desired measurement) and draw a line through the crow's foot with a speed square.

3. Cut your wood to 24" (or whatever measurement you marked in step 2). If you are using a chop saw, you must know how to use one and have an adult nearby. If you are using a handsaw or jigsaw, you must also know how to use it, and have an adult nearby, but we'll give you a few tips. Using clamps, attach the wood to the work surface so the line you marked hangs over the table by at least 4", leaving the majority of the wood on the table.

4. For a handsaw: Place your nondominant hand on the portion of the board still on the table.

5. Place the handsaw on your line, holding it with your dominant hand. Begin by sliding it along your line lightly and quickly. Do this over and over, and slowly the saw will begin to cut. Saw until the extra wood falls to the ground.

6. It's now time to mark the holes to drill. Lay your 24" board on the work surface. Using your tape measure, from the short end of the board, measure 3", and mark the point with a crow's foot. Using your speed square, draw a line through the crow's foot, from one long end of the board to the other.

7. From the long end of the board, measure 1½" and 4" along the line you've just drawn, and mark it with a crow's foot.

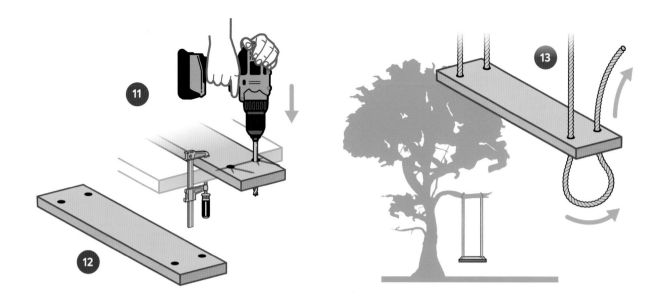

8. Repeat steps 6 and 7 on the other short end of the board. The four crow's feet you've marked are your drill points.

9. Get out your drill and insert the ⅝" bit into the end, tightening the drill bit snugly into the drill.

10. Making sure the 2x6 is secured with either an adult's help or clamps, place the tip of the bit onto any of the four crow's feet you marked on your 3" line. Take one quick look under the 2x6 to ensure that your drill isn't going to drill through the board and into your work surface. If all is good, move on to the next step.

11. With the drill secure, hit the trigger, and bore a hole through the 2x6 until you come out the other side. Run the drill up and down a few times to make sure the hole is clean and free of wood bits.

12. Repeat this step on the remaining four drill points; your board will have two holes on each end.

13. It's time to run the rope through the swing. Cut your rope to length using your heavy-duty scissors. (If your measurements were right when you bought your rope, this means you should cut your rope in half.) Have an adult burn the ends of your rope if they are not already burned. The rope can melt and drip, so keep bare skin away from burning rope. To push the ropes through the holes, you might need to twist the rope.

14. Next, find a good, thick branch to which you can attach your swing. Search the internet for how to tie knots, or ask an adult for a lesson on how to best secure your ropes to the tree, then the ropes to the swing.

15. Once your swing is all tied up, hop on, kick those legs, and have a grand old time!

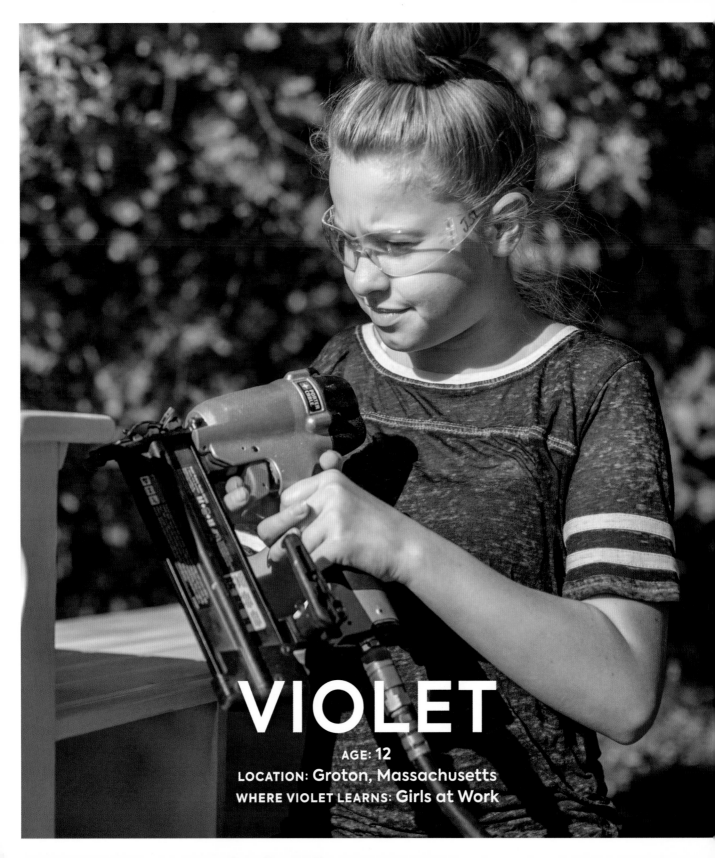

VIOLET

AGE: **12**
LOCATION: **Groton, Massachusetts**
WHERE VIOLET LEARNS: **Girls at Work**

> *The possibilities are endless, and you can make and design whatever you put your mind to!*

What are some things you want us to know about you?

I started building when I was nine, and I also play saxophone and make crafts.

What is the first thing you ever built?

The first thing I built was a little chair when I was around seven. I built it with my grandpa, and I was really proud of it.

How does building make you feel?

Building makes me feel really smart and powerful because when I start a project I always start with an idea, and as I work on it I think, "This would be so much cooler if I added this here or changed the length of it here."

Why do you build?

I build so I can personalize and make anything, and so I can inspire other girls to do the same.

What advice do you have for other girls?

Sometimes it gets really hard and you feel like giving up, and that's okay. You can take a break and then get back to work, and building involves so much creative problem-solving.

What's the first step in trying something new?

For me it's just believing I can do it and persevering.

Who do you look up to?

I look up to so many people in my life and people I've never met. They're all so inspiring to me because they remind me of what I have ahead of me and how many struggles I've overcome.

What are some other activities that make you feel courageous, strong, and bold?

I love to try new things.

What are some ideas of things girls can build at home?

I always like to make personal things as gifts, like customized shelves, little (or big!) step stools, or benches. The possibilities are endless, and you can make and design whatever you put your mind to!

What project are you sharing with us?

A bench I made this summer.

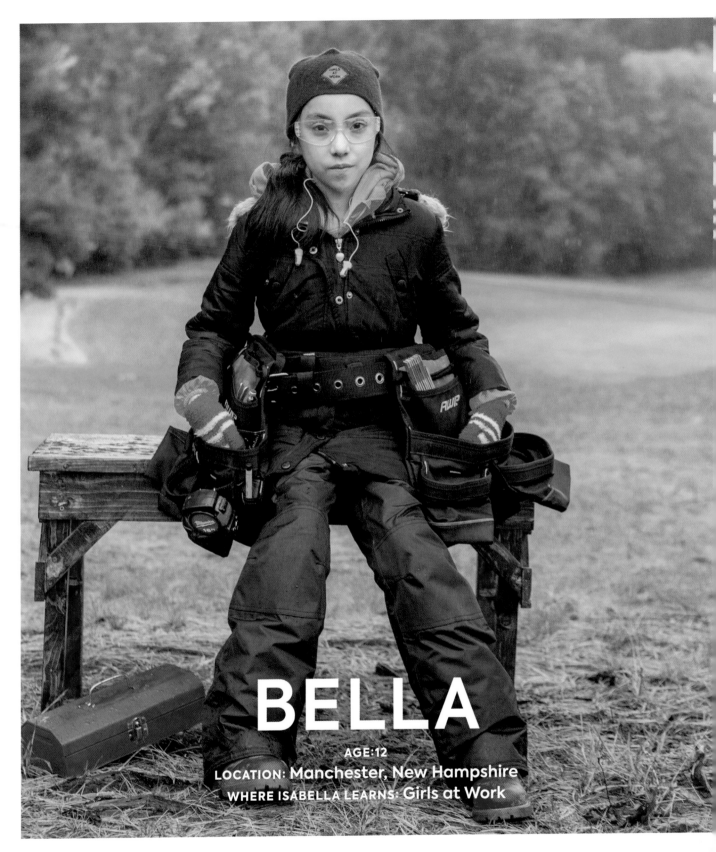

BELLA

AGE:12
LOCATION: Manchester, New Hampshire
WHERE ISABELLA LEARNS: Girls at Work

*" Building makes me feel that
I can do anything that comes my way. "*

What are some things you want us to know about you?
I love to build, and I enjoy making stuff like headbands and bracelets.

What is the first thing you ever built?
The first thing I built that came from my head was a coffee table. I built it for my house so when I see it I can tell myself, "I built this."

How does building make you feel?
Building makes me feel that I can do anything that comes my way.

Why do you build?
I build to teach myself that I am in control.

What advice do you have for other girls?
To stay strong and never give up.

What's the first step in trying something new?
To start it and don't quit until it is done.

Who do you look up to?
I look up to my parents because they taught me how to be respectful.

What are some other activities that make you feel courageous, strong, and bold?
Student government, to show that I can lead others.

What are some ideas of things girls can build at home?
Pegboard, shelf, box.

What project are you sharing with us?
A coffee table.

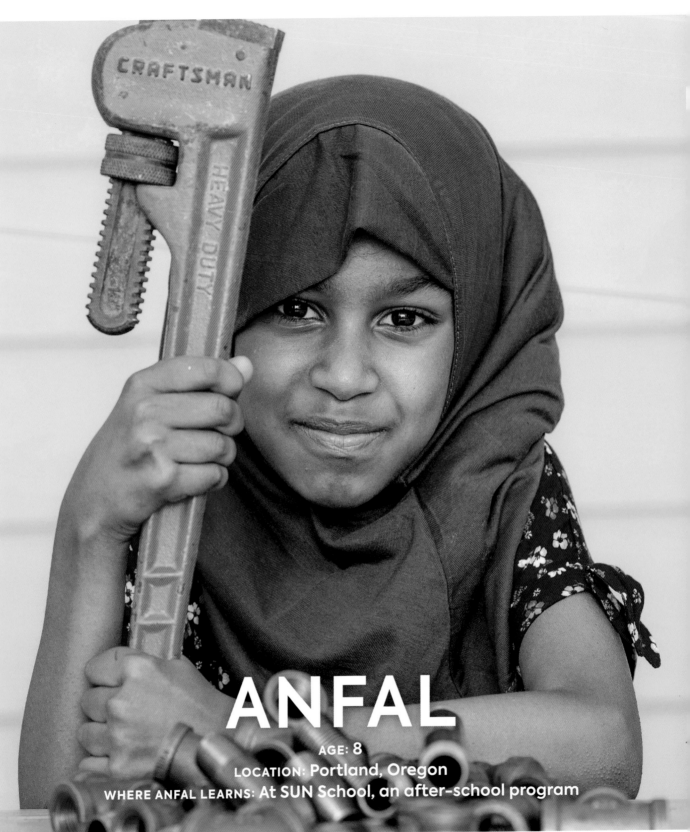

ANFAL

AGE: 8
LOCATION: Portland, Oregon
WHERE ANFAL LEARNS: At SUN School, an after-school program

> *Be brave.*
> *Because life is not that scary.*

What are some things you want us to know about you?

I like making play dough, and I love making slime, especially orange, pink, and blue. I like to play tag with Khadija. I was born in Portland, and I live with my mom and my dad and my two baby brothers. I like PE because I like running. I speak Swahili, Somali, and English. Orange is my favorite color. I like birds, especially jays because they are blue, my old favorite color. We learned about birds in science, and we got to make bird feeders. I like to play in the snow. We had a snowball fight against the boys.

What is the first thing you ever built?

A playground in art class out of paper. We had hopscotch, slides, and a tunnel. We got to put it in a green screen, and we put grass and a picture of something on the green screen. And the playground was big on the green screen. My friend and I put our two playgrounds together, and it was one big playground.

How does building make you feel?

Good. It is fun to use the wrenches. You get to make cool stuff.

Why do you build?

Because building is fun and I wanted to do it again after I got to do it at school.

What advice do you have for other girls?

Be brave. Because life is not that scary.

What's the first step in trying something new?

You can do it with a friend.

Who do you look up to?

My mom and my dad.

What are some other activities that make you feel courageous, strong, and bold?

When I went on my first roller-coaster I was really scared, and it got funner and funner and funner.

What are some ideas of things girls can build at home?

A bridge out of toilet paper rolls or Popsicle sticks. A scarf.

What project are you sharing with us?

I built a candleholder made out of pipes.

ANFAL'S CANDLEHOLDER

Anfal put this project together outside her apartment building in a shared playground and grassy area. She had to be quite protective of her tools and materials because when other kids came out to play they were really excited about what she was making. Her best friend, Khadija, was nearby working on her own project (see Project 2), and both girls were proud to show off their projects to their friends. One note: When buying the fittings for this project, buy one extra of each fitting, in case you accidentally grabbed the wrong one. People tend to mix them up at the store, and you don't want to have to come back! Also, you might need to special order the 4-way fitting.

MATERIALS

The following are all ½" gas pipe fittings:

- ❏ Six 90-degree elbows (Make sure you do not get street elbows. Double-check the label to make sure.)
- ❏ 5 tees
- ❏ Ten 2" nipples
- ❏ One 8" nipple
- ❏ One 4-way
- ❏ 5 taper candles

TOOLS

- ❏ 2 pipe wrenches

SKILLS

- ❏ Using a pipe wrench

> This project gets grease on your skin and clothes. Wear gloves if you want to, and be sure to have some rags nearby to clean your hands, clothes, etc.

Adult oversight:

Cost after tools:

Safety gear:
• Safety glasses
• Gloves (optional)

Work surface: Clean and flat—you don't want to lose parts

Skill level:

Time:

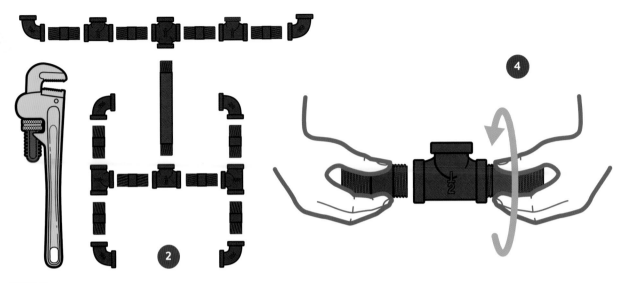

STEPS

1. Put on safety glasses and gloves. Check for and remove loose clothing and jewelry, and make sure hair is tied back. Put on gloves, if you are using them.

2. Lay out your pieces as shown in the diagram above.

3. You are going to want to put the pipes together in order, so start where it makes sense to you. Anfal started with the bottom left leg, then worked her way through from there.

4. Connect the pieces by hand. Place the end of one piece into the end of the piece lying next to it, then twist them together. You can connect many pieces this way and build small sections until all your pieces are used. Go through and

tighten one more time by hand. You can break the sections down however you want, but this is how Anfal put it together.

5. It's time to attach all the sections together to create one whole piece. Take a look at the drawing again, and start tightening sections together until your project looks like this.

6. You did a great job tightening your pieces by hand, but if you leave it like this, your candleholder will be wobbly. You need to tighten each piece with the pipe wrenches, like Anfal did. To tighten, place one piece in the mouth of a pipe wrench, making sure the mouth is closed around the fitting. Put the other pipe wrench on the next fitting, but facing the opposite direction. One wrench will hold the fitting in

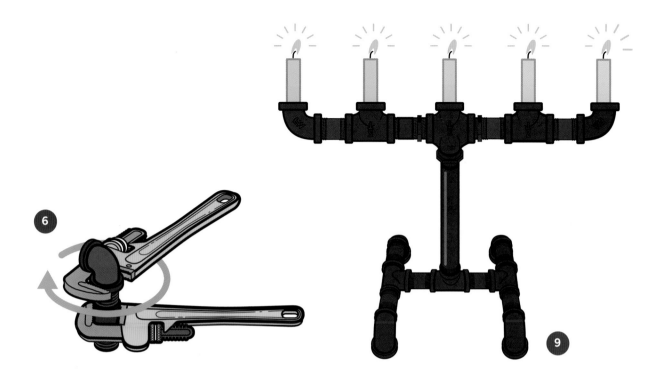

place while you rotate the other to tighten it. If the fitting slips in the pipe wrench, you need to either tighten the mouth of the wrench, or turn the wrench over so it grips the fitting correctly. Getting it right might take a few adjustments, and it may become frustrating, but that's okay. You are using a huge pipe wrench, and you should be pretty proud of yourself right now. You can 100 percent do this.

7. Grab an adult, because you'll need some extra muscles for this part. The hardest part of tightening is making sure that, as you tighten, you leave each piece in the right position, just like it was when you started. This might mean that you stop tightening a piece before it's as tight as you can get it so the piece remains upright. Take a minute to make sure all pieces are in the right positions.

8. There isn't a lot to this project. Simply keep fitting the pieces together and then tightening. The hardest part for Anfal was the top piece. It was difficult to get all the pieces lined up perfectly, but she was patient and got it aligned to her satisfaction.

9. Once the whole unit is assembled, go through and check that you didn't miss a piece while tightening. You want the candles to be secure at the top. Once everything is tight, your piece is complete. Push one candle into each opening at the top. Enjoy!

KALEAH

AGE: **11**

LOCATION: **Portland, Oregon**

WHERE KALEAH LEARNS: **Girls Build**

> *I build because it shows who I am and what I can be.*

What are some things you want us to know about you?

I have a cat named Carly. My favorite color is turquoise. Also, I like to spend my free time outside or with family. I have a brother and a sister, and my favorite subjects are math and science.

What is the first thing you ever built?

I built a mini bookshelf for my aunt and uncle.

How does building make you feel?

Building makes me feel like the person who I was meant to be. For example, when people ask if I've ever built something, I say that I went to a Girls Build camp.

Why do you build?

I build because it shows who I am and what I can be.

What advice do you have for other girls?

In the confrontation between the stream and the rock, the stream always wins, not from force, but through perseverance. The quote means that if you believe and persevere, you can achieve anything!

What's the first step in trying something new?

Just try it, and believe you can.

Who do you look up to?

My mom.

What are some activities that make you feel courageous, bold, and strong?

Hula, because it's my culture, and soccer, because it helps me to realize that there will always be someone supportive that's beside you.

What are some ideas of things girls can build at home?

Maybe a picture frame. Next, I want to build a combination cat house and play tower.

What project are you sharing with us?

A hanging shelving unit.

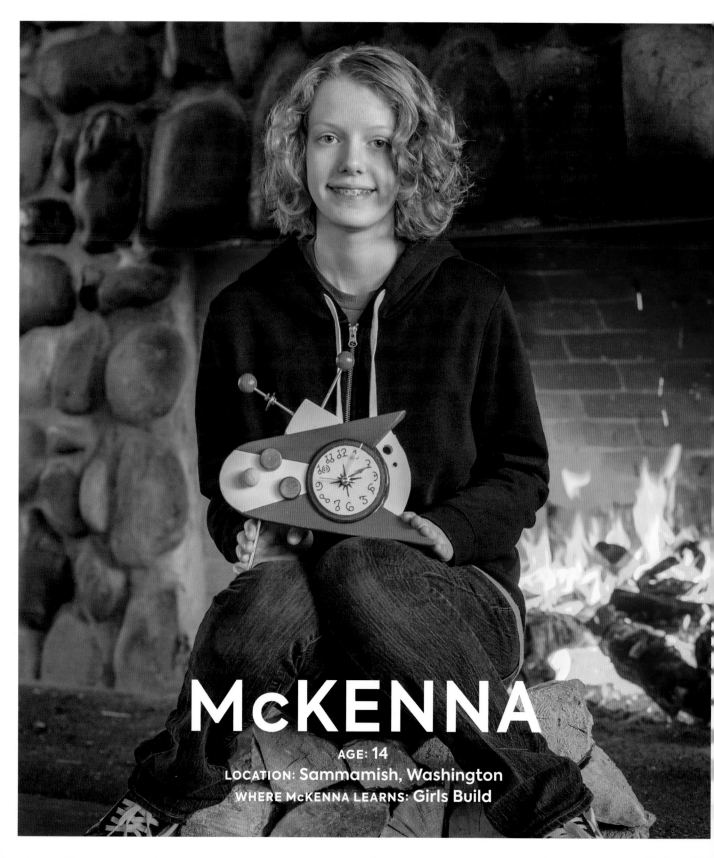

McKENNA

AGE: 14
LOCATION: Sammamish, Washington
WHERE McKENNA LEARNS: Girls Build

> *"No matter how big, crazy, or unrealistic something is, go for it."*

What are some things you want us to know about you?

I love hands-on projects. Art and music are my strengths, and I have a passion for retro science fiction and the history of technology (mainly the history of computers).

What is the first thing you ever built?

I built with Legos starting when I was three years old. I built with Legos because my dad gave his old Legos to me that he had when he was a kid.

How does building make you feel?

It makes me feel that I have a purpose in this world and makes me feel productive and accomplished. Building also satisfies my imagination.

Why do you build?

I build because I have the ability to and the imagination for it.

What advice do you have for other girls?

No matter how big, crazy, or unrealistic something is, go for it. If your imagination agrees with it, then you have the ability to bring it into reality.

What's the first step in trying something new?

Do a little research. Or jump in headfirst, and if you fail, you learn from it.

Who do you look up to?

I look up to the cofounder of Apple, Steve Wozniak. Because when he was a young boy he dreamed of having his own computer. He told his dad his dream, but his dad didn't believe in him. Wozniak followed his dream and his passion and with that created the Apple computer.

What are some other activities that make you feel courageous, strong, and bold?

Drawing/any form of art, playing music, researching the history of technology.

What are some ideas of things girls can build at home?

A birdhouse, small pieces of furniture (such as a coffee table), model buildings, a plant box, a cutting board.

What project are you sharing with us?

An analog table clock inspired by the style that the baby boomer generation thought the 21st century would be like.

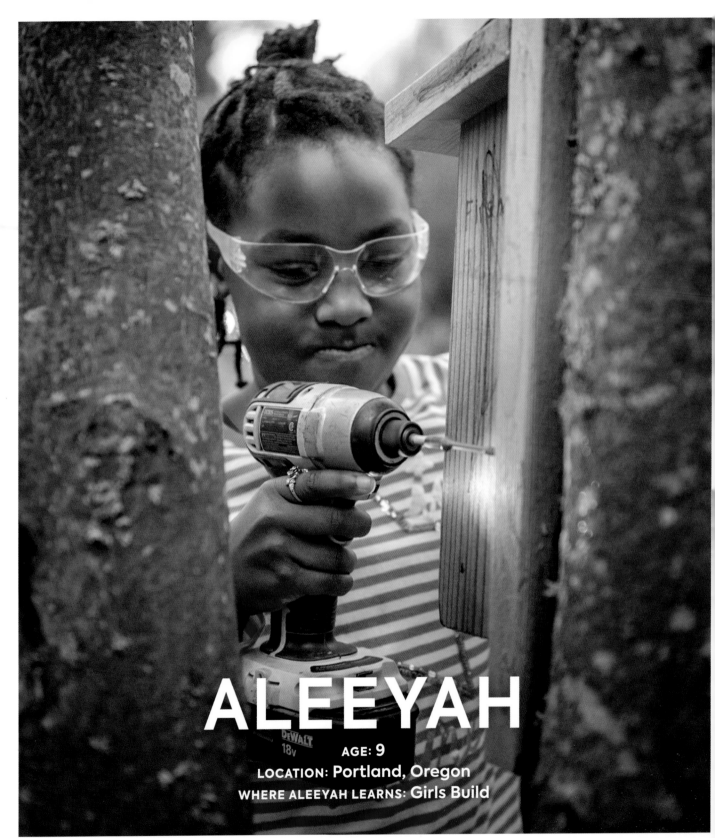

ALEEYAH

AGE: 9
LOCATION: Portland, Oregon
WHERE ALEEYAH LEARNS: Girls Build

Don't let people tell you that you can't do anything, or that you are weak.

What are some things you want us to know about you?

I do karate. I am in a youth group and we do community service. Also, I have a twin brother.

What is the first thing you ever built?

In pre-K I learned how to make a planter out of a milk carton.

How does building make you feel?

Building makes me feel independent. It makes me feel like that because you are able to build all by yourself.

Why do you build?

It is fun and relaxing. Also because it calms me when I am mad, sad, or frustrated, and sometimes I build to learn or to just have fun.

What advice do you have for other girls?

I want other girls to know to never stop dreaming. Also, don't let people tell you that you can't do anything, or that you are weak.

What's the first step in trying something new?

The first step is to see how it goes and how you feel about it.

Who do you look up to?

I look up to my mom and my older brothers and my older sister.

What other activities make you feel courageous, bold, and strong?

I like to sing, dance, and to teach.

What are some ideas of things girls can build at home?

Trays, hangers, a doghouse, a shed, and so many others.

What project are you sharing with us?

I built a mason bee house and I hung it on a tree in my front yard.

ALEEYAH'S
MASON BEE HOUSE

Aleeyah is a special kid whose laughter and intelligence put you at ease, as if you were chatting with a twenty-five-year-old. She welcomed us into her home, where she built her mason bee house in her backyard. She's clearly comfortable in front of a camera. We captured both hysterical laughter and her serious work face. This kid is going places.

MATERIALS

- ❑ One 4x4x8 board, *not* cedar or juniper
- ❑ One 1x6x8 cedar board
- ❑ Twelve 1½" exterior screws
- ❑ Masking tape or blue tape

> Cedar 1x6 boards can crack easily. It is best to predrill holes before you drive in screws, and don't screw near the edges of the wood—they will split, and you'll be sad.

TOOLS

- ❑ Tape measure
- ❑ Pencil
- ❑ Speed square
- ❑ Chop saw
- ❑ Drill
- ❑ ⁵⁄₁₆" drill bit
- ❑ ⅛" drill bit
- ❑ Drill bit that matches your screws
- ❑ 2 bar clamps (optional; you can ask a buddy to help you instead)
- ❑ Sander (optional)
- ❑ Ruler

SKILLS

- ❑ Measuring
- ❑ Sawing
- ❑ Drilling

Adult oversight:

Cost after tools:

Safety gear:
- Safety glasses
- Ear protection

Work surface: Sturdy and flat

Skill level:

Time:

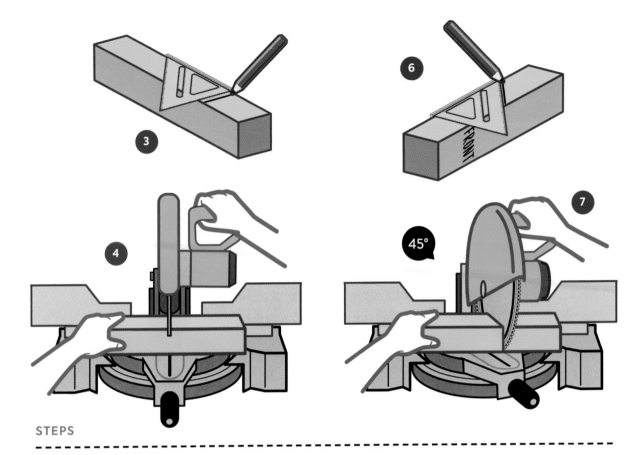

STEPS

1. Put on safety glasses and ear protection. Check for and remove loose clothing and jewelry, and make sure hair is tied back.

2. Take a look at your two boards. One is a very long square (the 4x4), and one is a very long rectangle (the 1x6). Become familiar with these sizes, so you can easily grab the 4x4 when it is called out, and likewise the 1x6. If you don't pay attention, you will cut the wrong board.

3. Measure 12" on your 4x4, and mark a crow's foot. Draw a line through the crow's foot with your speed square.

4. Now you need to use a chop saw, so ask an experienced adult to help you. Use the chop saw to cut the board to your line (on the waste side of your line), creating a 12" block.

5. Determine which side of the 4x4 you want to be the front. This is simply a matter of which side you like most. Write "front" in large letters on the side you have chosen.

6. From one end of the 4x4 (your choice), use the speed square to draw a 45-degree angle so the lowest point is on the front (see illustration).

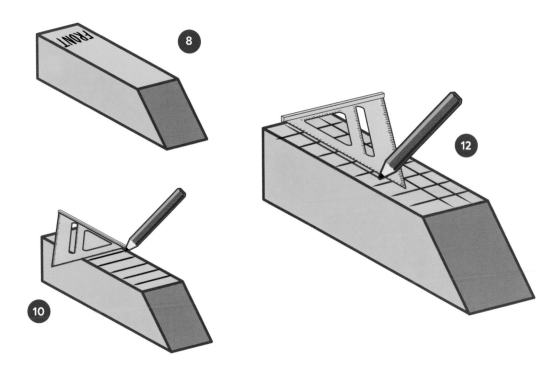

7. Cut the 4x4 on the 45-degree-angle line by rotating the table of the chop saw to 45 degrees. Remember to keep your hands and arms parallel to the blade, and keep your fingers a safe distance from the blade. It is best to cut the board with the waste side to the right of the blade.

8. Once the cut is complete, lay the wood on a stable surface with the front facing up. The back should now be longer than the front.

9. You are about to make a grid across the front of your board. Hook your tape measure on the bottom of your board. Mark a crow's foot at every inch mark (at 2", 3", 4", etc.).

10. Use your speed square to draw lines across the front at every inch mark.

11. Going in the opposite direction across the narrow face of the board (the bottom), mark crow's feet at ¾", 1¾", and 2¾".

12. At each of the crow's feet you just marked, use your speed square and ruler to draw lines along the front of the board, so you have three lines running vertically up the face of the board. You now have a grid of pencil lines covering the front of the 4x4.

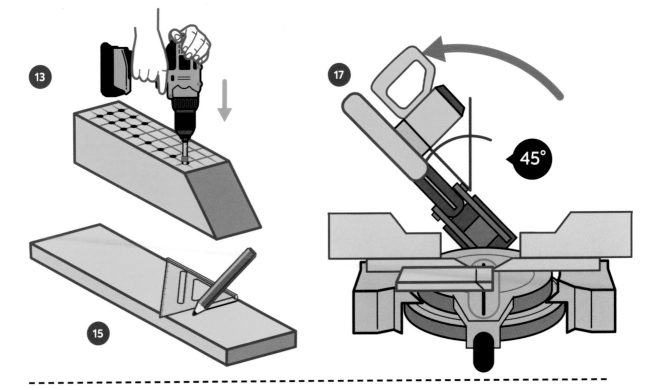

13. Now you need to mark the depth of the hole on the bit. Lay your bit on the work surface and then measure 3" from the tip of the bit. At the 3" mark, wrap tape all the way around the bit. Make it nice and dark. When you drill the holes for this step, make sure you don't go past your tape, and you will be fine.

14. Where the lines intersect, use the ⁵⁄₁₆" bit to bore holes *almost* all the way through the 4x4, stopping when the face of the wood meets the edge of the tape. Once the holes are complete, set the 4x4 aside.

15. Next, get out the cedar 1x6. Measure 16" along the long side of the board, mark a crow's foot, and use your speed square to draw a line across the board.

16. Cut the 1x6 on your measured line at 16". Write "back" on this piece (on either side), and set it aside.

17. On the remaining portion of the 1x6, measure 6" from one end. Mark a crow's foot, and draw a 90-degree line with your speed square across the face of the board. Move the 1x6 to the chop saw. Adjust the blade on the saw so it will make a 45-degree beveled cut along the narrow edge of the 1x6. Cut the board at the 6" line you marked. This cut should be done by someone with a lot of experience on the chop saw. Make sure you keep your hands far from the blade.

18. Once the cut is complete, set the piece aside. This will be your 6" piece.

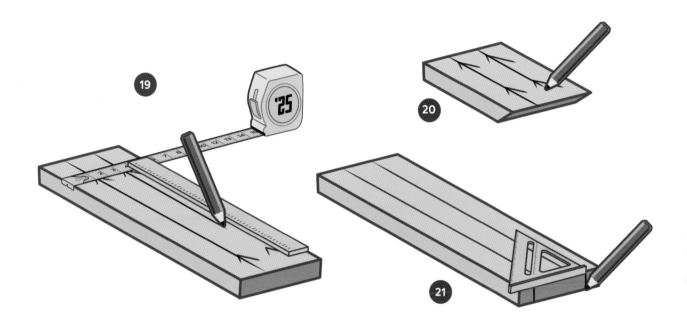

19. To make two lines up the length of your 1x6, lay your 16" 1x6 on your work surface. Along the narrow end of the back of the board, measure and mark 2¼" and 3¼". On the opposite narrow end, make two more crow's feet at 2¼" and 3¼". Using your speed square, draw lines vertically up the 1x6, connecting the crow's feet with a ruler, piece of wood, or the edge of your speed square.

20. Now make the same measurements on the 6" piece, drawing lines perpendicular to the cut side, with the short end of the angle facing down. Next, measure along each line you just drew, marking crow's feet at each line at 2" and 5".

21. On the 16" 1x6, write "front" on the side without lines. Along the narrow end of the board, again draw two crow's feet, 1" from each side.

You actually want to draw lines along the tiny, narrow edge of the board. You can mark this easily by measuring the face, then marking on the short, narrow end where the wide side of the speed square goes over the edge, giving you a straight edge to mark. These mark where your 4x4 will sit in order to be attached to the 1x6.

22. Get out the drill and put the ⅛" bit in it. Set out the screws, and get the bit out that will drive the screws.

23. Set the 4x4 on a stable surface near the drills and screws, hole-side down. Lay the 16" 1x6 on top of the 4x4 so the bottoms are *flush*, front-side down. Make sure the 4x4 is between the lines you've drawn on the front and edge of the 1x6.

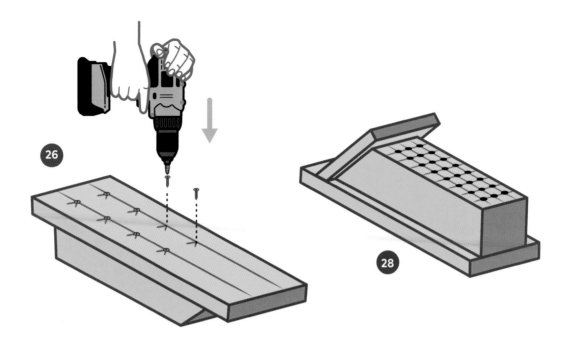

24. Have your buddy, or a set of clamps, gently hold the 1x6 on the 4x4 securely as you get ready to predrill your screw holes, making sure the bottoms of the 1x6 and the 4x4 stay flush with each other. Near the top, slide your tape measure under the 1x6, and make sure the edge of the 1x6 is at the 1" mark. If it's not, do a slight adjustment to make it 1". This ensures that the spacing is equal at the top and bottom along the sides.

25. Drill four holes about 1½" deep along each line of the 1x6, evenly spaced, but no closer than 1" to the top or bottom of the board. If you would like more precise measurements, Aleeyah's holes are at 1½", 4¼", 6¾", and 9".

26. Switch your bits so you are ready to drive screws. Drive one screw into each hole you just drilled. If it feels more comfortable, clamp the whole unit to the work surface while you're driving the screws, making sure your pieces stay flush and even.

27. Turn the board over. You are now ready to install the roof.

28. Fit the 6" piece of 1x6 snugly into the angled spot between the 4x4 and the long 1x6 so the lines you have drawn are faceup. The angle you cut earlier will butt up against the 16" board.

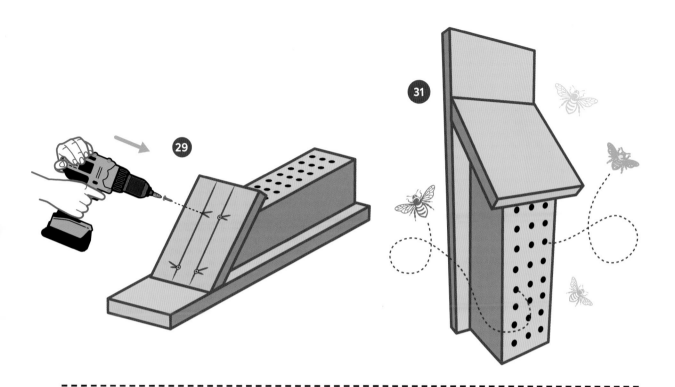

29. Switch your bits so you have the ⅛" bit ready in your drill. It might be helpful to reclamp your bee house to the table, or you can have your buddy hold the 6" 1x6 in place. Bore four holes through the roof on the crow's feet you marked earlier.

30. Next, switch bits, and drive four screws into the holes you just created.

31. You may now sand your bee house if you choose. It is complete! Bees need a little help finding out which hole is theirs. If you want to, add some color next to each hole to help the bees find their homes.

32. To attach the bee house to a tree or post, drill a hole in the center of the wood above the roof, at least 1" from the top. Next, grab a long screw, pick a final home for your bee house, and drive a screw through the hole and into the tree or post.

33. Congratulations! You are the owner of a homemade bee house!

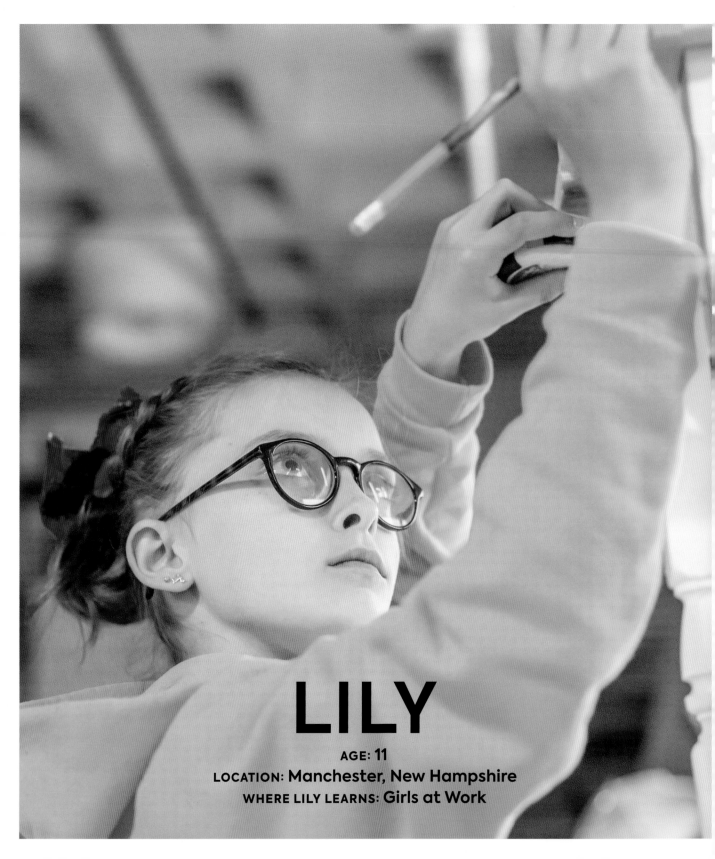

LILY

AGE: 11
LOCATION: Manchester, New Hampshire
WHERE LILY LEARNS: Girls at Work

> ❝ *Building makes me feel happy, calm, and, most of all, cheerful.* ❞

What are some things you want us to know about you?

I'm an honor-roll student. I cheerlead, snowboard, have danced for eight years, and I am a rock-star builder with Girls at Work! This year I even led hundreds of high schoolers in a career-day pegboard project.

What is the first thing you ever built?

My first build was a pegboard. By now I have made at least five of these as they are great for storing cheer bows and hats, and as last-minute gifts.

How does building make you feel?

Building makes me feel happy, calm, and, most of all, cheerful. I can be having a bad day, and then I go to Girls at Work and get around the people and start building, and I feel so much better.

Why do you build?

I like working with wood and having something to show for my work. I really like being a leader, though. Since last summer I have learned how to build large pieces and teach others to build as well.

What advice do you have for other girls?

If people tell you that you can't, do the opposite!

What's the first step in trying something new?

Be safe, and go for it!

Who do you look up to?

My mommy because she is always there for me, no matter my mood, and Ms. Elaine from Girls at Work because she has given us a place to learn and grow. She doesn't judge us, and she cares. Ms. Elaine was told she couldn't be a builder because she was a girl.

She was told to be a secretary, and she said, "Forget that" and did it her way.

What are some other activities that make you feel courageous, strong, and bold?

Snowboarding, flying in cheer, and even though it's super girly, I love ballet. I just feel really strong when I am doing physical things.

What are some ideas of things girls can build at home?

Treasure boxes, lap desks, stools. It doesn't have to be complicated.

What project are you sharing with us?

I made a table so that when I have my own room I can decorate it with my furniture that I custom made.

GABII

AGE: 8
LOCATION: New Orleans, Louisiana
WHERE GABII LEARNS: Electric Girls

> *Building makes me feel like I can do whatever I want,*
> *because I can do whatever I want.*

What are some things you want us to know about you?

I am a very fun person. I am very energetic. At times I can be a little bit crazy like yelling a lot and dancing and jumping off of things. And I enjoy mocha Frappuccinos, but they're decaf. I enjoy sports and play soccer and basketball. I am trying out for tennis and I play violin. I enjoy art—I draw things that I see. The last thing I painted was a lady watching over a house that seemed old, and in the back was a rainbow. When I relax, I just sit on the couch and draw, or just take a nap. I like taking pictures of things on my iPad; then I put specific filters on them, and they are really beautiful.

What is the first thing you ever built?

The first thing I built was a house made of foam, and then I drew on it, and made a couch and a TV. It wasn't that big so it only had a living room. It was a house for ants and I put it on my front porch. And I found a caterpillar that had made a cocoon in there, so it could turn into a butterfly. I was six when I built it.

How does building make you feel?

Building makes me feel like I can do whatever I want, because I *can* do whatever I want. I can be creative in my own way, and I can just do anything.

Why do you build?

I build so that I can stay creative, keep doing my art, because I want to keep that up throughout the years. I want to do different types of art, and building can be one of them.

What advice do you have for other girls?

Be creative, do what you love to do, don't let other people tell you what you need to do.

What's the first step in trying something new?

If it is your first time trying something, you can go ahead and do it, and you can change it—you can do it your own way. If you're nervous, think about it first. Is this really what I want to do? Make up your mind, breathe a little bit, then try it. And if you don't like it, just try something different.

Who do you look up to?

Usually I look up to my mom. She is very creative. She doesn't listen to other people. She does things her own way and she's very fun. I love her.

What are some other activities that make you feel courageous, strong, and bold?

Dance, because it makes me feel like I can express myself. You can create your own dance, and then dance it on the stage. I dance ballet and modern dance. Also violin, because with violin you can make your own song, and when you perform your song you're doing your own thing—it's you being yourself the whole time.

What are some ideas of things girls can build at home?

They can really build anything. They can build a house out of paper, out of origami, or out of tape. Give it a roof made out of paper. Or a house made of cardboard. Or a cat made out of cardboard. They can build things out of straws so they don't throw away straws, and that way they can save the sea turtles. You can reuse plastic and use it to build something. Like, if you had a to-go box, you can make it into a huge monster's mouth, and then you can chomp people.

What project are you sharing with us?

I am going to build a soccer tournament. The whole stadium and people who can move around and kick a soccer ball, and say things like GOALLLLLLLLLLLL!

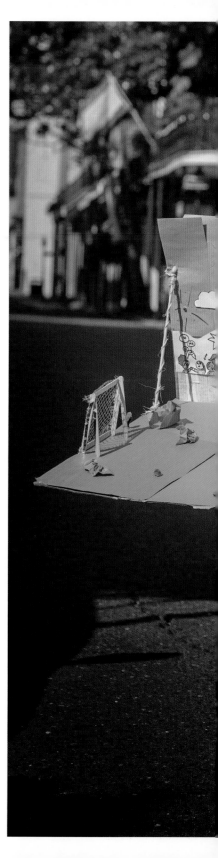

SOLEIL

AGE: 8
LOCATION: Cabo San Lucas, Mexico
WHERE SOLEIL LEARNS: At home and at school

> *[Building] is fun and you can always have new stuff and you can build whatever you want.*

What are some things you want us to know about you?

I love elephants and I love the color blue. And if any animal is hurt I want to save it. I'm funny.

What is the first thing you ever built?

I built a car out of a giant box because I wanted to learn how to drive. I also built a doghouse for my dog Charly.

How does building make you feel?

Building things makes me feel like I'm a builder and I feel good.

Why do you build?

Because it's fun and you can always have new stuff and you can build whatever you want.

What advice do you have for other girls?

Build easy and then go up, bigger from there. Always have fun.

What is the first step in trying something new?

First step is to be excited and try new things, and then you can be good at it.

Who do you look up to?

American dancer JoJo Siwa. Because she is always happy, she helps people, and she gets to go on tour.

What other activities make you feel courageous, strong, and bold?

Doing my school shows, helping an animal get better, saving a bee from the swimming pool.

What are some things girls can build at home?

A picture frame, a desk, a box for toys.

What project are you sharing with us?

I built a magnet board. I am going to put my school stuff on it and pictures that I drew.

SOLEIL'S MAGNET BOARD

Soleil built her magnet board on the beach after school one day. She had a small portable work surface and a battery-operated drill and jigsaw. Soleil was fierce and excited, and she wore a denim dress with cut-off sleeves and a sequined image of a slice of pepperoni pizza on the front, which I loved. Soleil interrupted her building by dancing on the rocks and occasionally running at the ocean while yelling.

MATERIALS

- ❑ At least 18″ of 1x6 pine (or similar wood)
- ❑ 24 narrow and thin wood slats (⅛″–¼″ thick)—for example, paint stir sticks, rulers, yardsticks, lath, etc.
- ❑ Two hundred fifty-five ¾″ ceramic magnets (about 6 bags, available at hardware or craft stores)
- ❑ About eighty ¾″ nails (You can have some fun with your nails, since they will be visible. You could use silver, black, or even copper nails!)
- ❑ 2 triangle ring hangers (aka picture hangers) with nails or screws (which usually come with the hangers).

TOOLS

- ❑ ¾″ Forstner bit (Soleil used a spade bit because a Forstner bit was not easily available in Cabo San Lucas. You can use a spade bit, but a Forstner bit is easier, cleaner, and safer.)
- ❑ Black marker
- ❑ Tape measure
- ❑ Pencil
- ❑ Speed square
- ❑ Two bar clamps
- ❑ Jigsaw or circular saw
- ❑ Drill or drill press
- ❑ Hammer
- ❑ Ruler

SKILLS

- ❑ Hammering
- ❑ Drilling
- ❑ Clamping
- ❑ Measuring
- ❑ Sawing

Adult oversight:

Cost after tools:

Safety gear:
- Safety glasses
- Ear protection

Work surface: Flat table or workbench

Skill level:

Time:

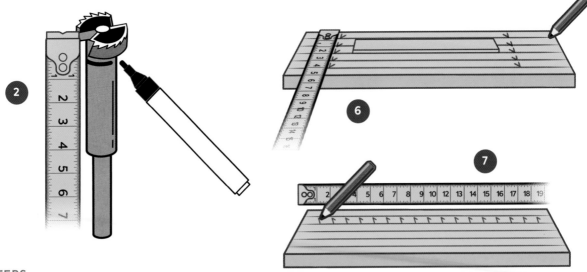

STEPS

1. Put on safety glasses and ear protection. Check for and remove loose clothing and jewelry, and make sure hair is tied back.

2. Lay out your Forstner bit, your marker, and your tape measure. Open your tape measure to about 6", and lock it. Now, hook your tape to the bottom of the bit. Using your black marker, draw a line on your bit at ⅝". Draw the line all the way around the bit.

3. Measure your 1x6 to 24", mark it with a crow's foot, and draw a line through the crow's foot using your speed square and pencil.

4. If using a jigsaw, clamp your wood to the work surface with the line you drew hanging over the edge. This way, when you cut the wood the extra piece can fall freely to the ground.

5. Cut the wood on the line, using the saw of your choice.

6. Measuring from the long end of the 24" board, close to one of the short ends, hook the tape measure on the edge of the board and make crow's feet at ¾", 1¾", 2¾", 3¾", and 4¾". Do the same close to the other short end of the board. Use your speed square to draw lines lengthwise along the board. You will have a gap between the lines, so use your ruler or one of your slats to connect the lines.

7. Measuring along the long end of the board, make a crow's foot at every inch (1"–23"). Using your speed square, draw a line across the board at each crow's foot. Your board should now be marked up with a grid of nice, straight pencil lines.

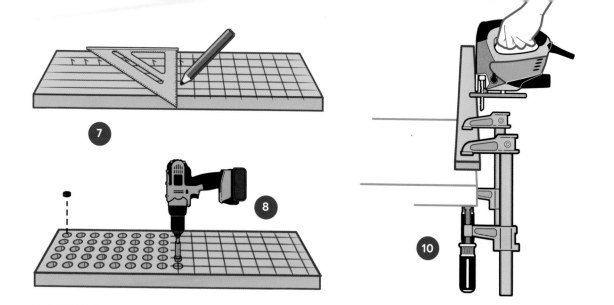

8. Where the lines intersect, you will drill holes for your magnets. Clamp the wood securely to the work surface. Insert the ¾" Forstner bit into your drill. Using two hands correctly placed (see "How to Drill"), carefully set the center of the bit on the first intersection, and drill into the wood until just the top of the black line you marked on the bit is showing. Do this at every intersection. If you are using a drill press, you will set the drill press up so the table is close to the bit and the bit is centered on a cross point. Clamp the wood to the table of the drill press, turn the press on, then lower the bit into the wood. Adjust for each new hole.

9. Take a moment to admire the beautiful holes you just drilled in that 24" board. It's time to test each hole for depth. Get out two magnets and drop them into your first hole. If your hole is not deep enough for both, drill the hole a little deeper to create the correct depth. You can remove the magnets by placing another magnet on top and then lifting all three out. Once you have determined that each hole is deep enough, set the board aside.

10. It is time to cut your wooden slats to length. Soleil decided to make her slats 10" long, and to arrange them in a staggered pattern that she liked. We are going to copy Soleil's idea here, but you can be creative with how your wood slats are laid out. To copy Soleil, measure each wooden slat to 10" using your tape measure, pencil, and speed square. Cut each slat to 10" using the jigsaw or chop saw. If you use the jigsaw, you want to clamp the wood to the work surface, keeping the line close to the edge of the work surface. To figure out how many slats you need, divide 24" by the width of the slat. (Soleil needed 17.) The slats can overhang a little on the ends if that's how the sizing works out (no need to cut the boards narrower).

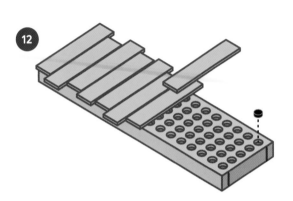

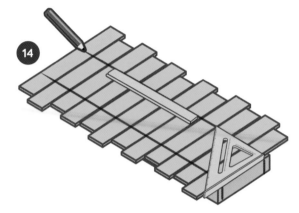

11. On the narrow edge of your 1x6, measure out ¼" and 5⅛" (you will have to burn an inch, which means you will be marking at 1¼" and 6⅛"). Using your speed square, mark down the edge of your board. Repeat these marks on the opposite end of your board.

12. Place your 24" board with the drilled holes on the work surface. Lay the slats of wood over the holes, arranging them in a pattern of your choosing.

13. If you are staggering your slats like Soleil's, the easiest way to make sure the slats stay even as you cross your board is to measure a 1" overhang on one side of each slat as you go.

14. Once the 10" slats are laid out, it's time to mark where you will drive your nails. You have only a few spots to drive nails where you won't run into a magnet. Lay your speed square so the wide edge is tight against the edge. Line your speed square up with your existing marks and draw a line across your slats. See illustration 14. Repeat on the remaining three lines so you have four marks across your boards. Connect the lines with the ruler.

15. Next, remove one or two 10" slats, get your magnets, and drop two magnets into each exposed hole. The magnets, which are attracted to the other magnets, will want to jump out of their holes, but work slowly and patiently. Work to get three rows of magnets

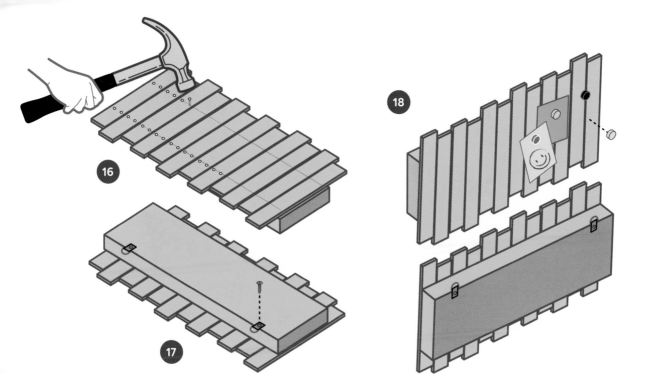

in, then install your first slat (next step). If your slats are narrower than Soleil's, you might only need to fill two rows before one slat will fully cover them.

16. Lay your slat on top of the magnets you have installed in the holes. Make sure your marks line up with the rest of the nail lines on your board. Get out your nails and drive in two nails on each end of the slat, using the nail lines you drew as your guides. Alternate between laying magnets and installing the slats one slat at a time. This will minimize the magnets jumping out of their holes.

17. Once you've finished nailing, turn your board over, slat-side down. Get out your trian-

gle ring hangers. The magnet board will hang horizontally—that is, with the long sides at the top and bottom. Place a ring hanger at the top of the 1x6, about 2" from the left side. Align the small rectangle that sits below the triangle with the top of the 1x6. Use the nails or screws that came with the hanger to install it. Make sure the rectangle stays even with the top of the board. Install the other hanger on the right side, 2" from the edge.

18. You now have a completed magnet board! Soleil is using hers to stick notes and pictures. You can use anything metal to stick pictures and paper to your board—nuts and washers, paper clips, barrettes, etc. Have fun!

AZALEA

AGE: **8**
LOCATION: **Portland, Oregon**
WHERE AZALEA LEARNS: **At home**

> *I build so I can tell men that women can also build.*

What are some things you want us to know about you?

I am calm. I have a twin brother. I like to be around people who are calm.

What is the first thing you ever built?

I built with a Lego set, and I made a clay pot with little balls in it.

How does building make you feel?

It makes me feel excited and happy.

Why do you build?

I build so I can tell men that women can also build.

What advice do you have for other girls?

That if they feel they can't build, or they are not allowed to, then they can. And if a boy says that you can't, then you ignore them and continue on.

What's the first step in trying something new?

Read the directions and follow the instructions.

Who do you look up to?

I look up to President Obama and Misty Copeland.

What other activities make you feel courageous, bold, and strong?

I feel courageous when I am patient and keep working even when it is hard. I feel good that next time I will be able to do it.

What are some ideas of things girls can build at home?

You could build a picture frame to hold a picture of someone who is really special to you—for example, your mom. You can also build a small house for your toys or a stuffed animal or even for a statue. You can also build a fake bed.

What project are you sharing with us?

I built a playhouse with Bailey and Zoélie.

BAILEY

AGE: 9
LOCATION: Portland, Oregon
WHERE BAILEY LEARNS: At home

> *Building might inspire you to be an architect when you grow up.*

What are some things you want us to know about you?

I'm from China. The first state I lived in was Arizona, and then I moved to Portland. I like to read a lot and do art in my basement. I cannot see with my left eye, and I have a prosthetic eye. It does not stop me from building because I can still see with my right eye. Even if you're blind in both eyes, you can still build!

What is the first thing you ever built?

Lots of Lego sets.

How does building make you feel?

Happy!

Why do you build?

It is one of my passions and I'm good at it.

What advice do you have for other girls?

Building might inspire you to be an architect when you grow up.

What's the first step in trying something new?

The first step is looking at the directions.

Who do you look up to?

I look up to my mom and my older sister.

What other activities make you feel courageous, bold, and strong?

Running and dancing.

What are some ideas of things girls can build at home?

Bridges and tiny houses.

What project are you sharing with us?

I built a playhouse with Azalea and Zoélie.

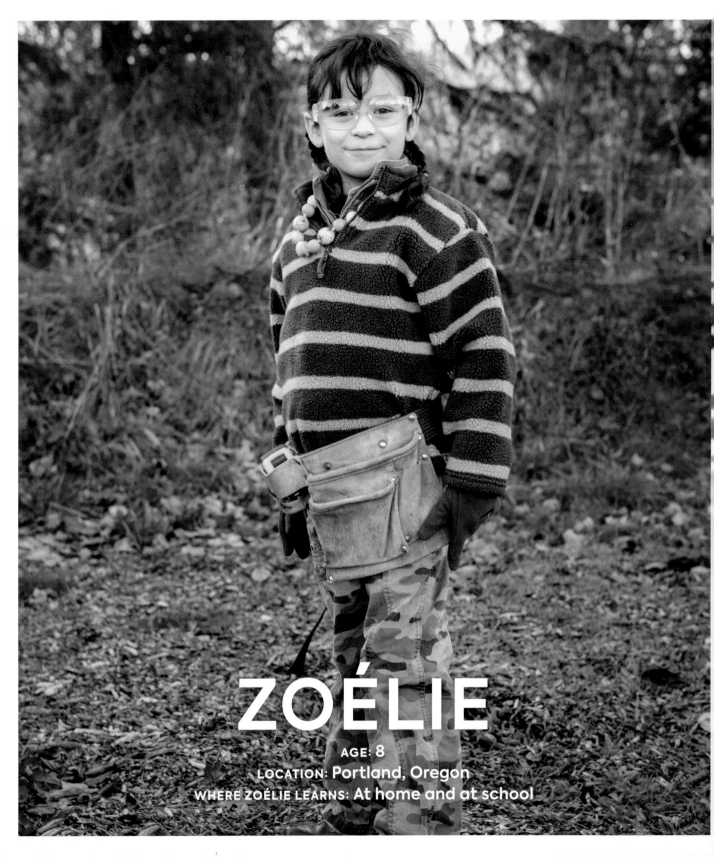

ZOÉLIE

AGE: 8
LOCATION: Portland, Oregon
WHERE ZOÉLIE LEARNS: At home and at school

> *I build to make the world change.*

What are some things you want us to know about you?

I am really creative in my heart. My head always invents new things.

What is the first thing you ever built?

I built a rolling toy dog out of empty toilet paper rolls, a small metal shopping cart, and wood sticks. I could pull him on a leash. I kept him for many years. I even took it to class for show and tell.

How does building make you feel?

It makes me feel creative and happy.

Why do you build?

I build to make the world change.

What advice do you have for other girls?

That boys can't tell you what to do.

What's the first step in trying something new?

You've got to think, then you've got to understand the materials you use. Then you need to invent it in your mind and see it in your mind. Then you don't really need instructions. Your mind is giving you the instructions.

Who do you look up to?

I am inspired by Michael Jackson and Prince, and by the builders who built the stages for them to perform.

What other activities make you feel courageous, strong, and bold?

Fighting for justice. I'm thinking of the thirteen girls [from Chelsea Clinton's book *She Persisted*, about 13 women who showed persistence and strength in the face of adversity] who changed the world when they persisted and didn't back down. The women did not do what was expected of them. They did something brave that made the world better. Sometimes being a girl isn't easy because some people will say that your dreams will definitely not happen. People say that you can't be an important person, that you can't be in history because you're a kid and a girl.

I want to help girls who are being told that they can't be powerful, that they are just "showing off," actually understand that they can be powerful and do things the way they want without being bossed around.

What are some ideas of things girls can build at home?

They can build chairs. A desk. Maybe they can even build little houses for animals and homes for the homeless.

What project are you sharing with us?

I built a playhouse with my sister Azalea and my friend Bailey.

AZALEA, BAILEY, AND ZOÉLIE'S PALLET PLAYHOUSE

Sisters Azalea and Zoélie spent the day with their friend Bailey out at a farm building this playhouse. It was incredibly cold, and the spirit of each of these girls shined through. Azalea meant business while her sister flitted about, measuring, lifting, and having a lot of fun. Bailey kept everyone's spirits up, the perfect balance of Azalea and Zoélie, laughing, working, and excited for the finished product. Since the girls used wood found around the farm, use these plans as a guide for your own—I guarantee it won't be exactly the same. Have fun!

MATERIALS

❏ Similarly sized rectangle pallets

❏ At least 6 pieces of lath, each at least 4' long (Note: The girls used lath because that is what they had on hand at the farm, but 2x4s will work even better than lath—you will need to adjust and use 3" screws instead of the 1½" screws if you use 2x4s.)

❏ About thirty-two 3" exterior screws

❏ Twenty 1½" exterior screws

❏ Twenty 3" exterior screws

❏ Extra to have on hand: up to five 2x4s, 4' to 5' long

TOOLS

❏ Drill

❏ Bits to match your screws

❏ Hammer

SKILLS

❏ Hammering

❏ Drilling

❏ Measuring

❏ Lifting

❏ A bit of creativity

All pallets are different and your playhouse may go together slightly differently than this one. Stick with the ideas, and make sure your playhouse is sturdy and safe.

Adult oversight:

Cost after tools:

Safety gear:
• Safety glasses
• Ear protection

Work surface: Any wide open and fairly flat area.

Skill level:

Time:

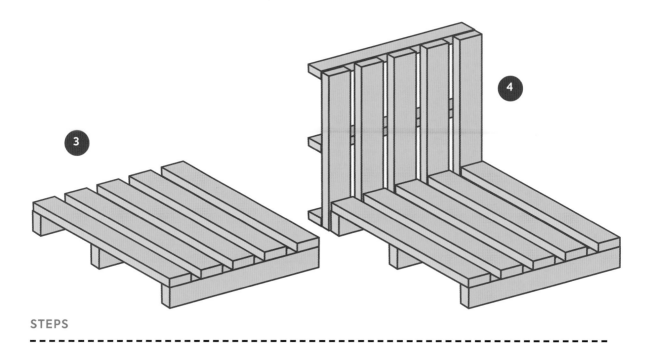

STEPS

1. Put on safety glasses and ear protection. Check for and remove loose clothing and jewelry, and make sure hair is tied back.

2. Have an adult check your pallets (wooden platforms) for nails that might poke out.

3. Pick a pallet with the most wood on it and lay it down where you want your playhouse to permanently reside. We will call this the "floor pallet."

4. If your pallets are rectangles, you will have a longer side and a shorter side. Pick a pallet for your first wall, and set it on one of its edges so it is lined up perpendicular to the floor pallet, going into the air. Make sure the lengths of the sides match or are close.

5. While one buddy holds that "wall pallet" in place up against the floor pallet, the other buddy can get the screws and get ready to attach the floor and wall together.

6. Look for spots where two pieces of the pallets meet so a screw can attach them. Drive a 3" screw through the wall pallet and into the floor pallet, with the screw parallel to the ground. Do this for a total of eight times, arranging the screws in a zigzag pattern. If

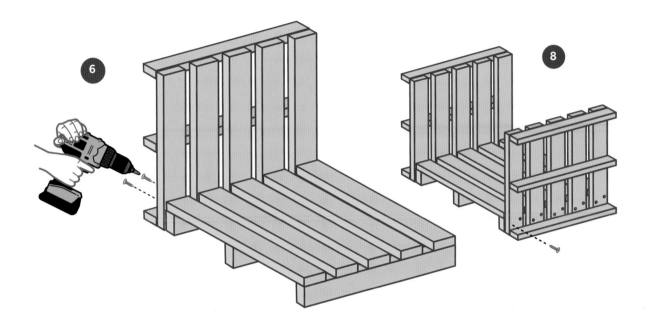

you are connecting two thin boards instead of two thick boards, you can use the 1½" screws instead. Tip: You may need to remove some boards in order to be able to get a drill in to drive a screw. See Cat's Paw on page 45.

7. Make sure the wall pallet feels somewhat secure before you move on. If not, put a few more screws in. Your wall will be a little wobbly. That's okay.

8. Go to the other side, and repeat steps 6 and 7 to attach another wall pallet to the floor pallet.

9. Decide which side will be the front of your playhouse and which side will be the back. Set the remaining pallet at the back, behind the floor pallet on the ground, with the long side on the ground so it overlaps the sidewalls. Attach the back wall pallet to the floor using the same steps you used to attach the sidewalls to the floor. Make sure all three wall pallets are flush with each other or are close to flush (not all pallets are exactly the same size). See illustration. Now attach the back wall pallet to each of the sidewall pallets, using several screws. You might need to toenail the screws to connect the wall pallets (see toenailing on page 39). Please note that our three girls used lath instead of a

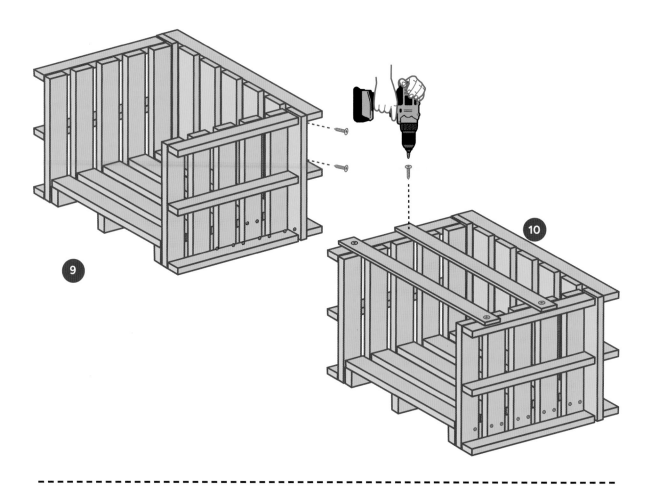

pallet for the back wall (even though a pallet is pictured here). Using lath for a wall is slightly more challenging and less sturdy, but the girls used what they had on hand. You could use 2x4s if this step is too challenging.

10. Optional: Now lay pieces of lath (as many as you'd like) across the top of the structure from one sidewall to the other. Using the 1½" screws, drive the screws through the lath and

into the wood of the pallets. If you'd like, instead of lath, you can use any long and sturdy wood you find, and you can make the roof more solid, if you'd like, by using more pieces of wood.

11. If you skipped step 10, you must now lay one piece of lath or 2x4 across the front of the playhouse to secure the walls to each other. See illustration 10.

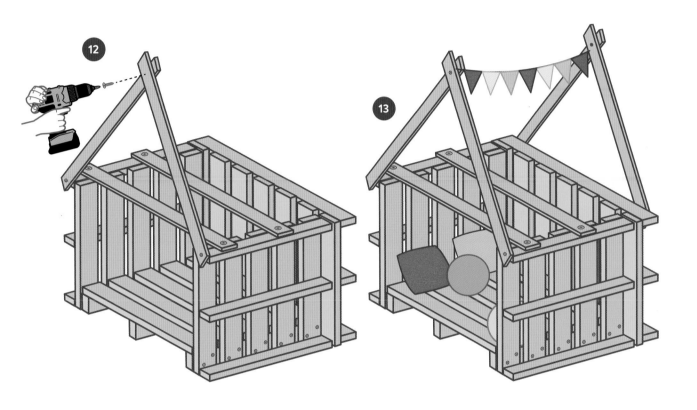

12. Once the walls are secure, you may now create an A-framed "roof." Azalea, Zoélie, and Bailey chose to use two pieces of lath to create the idea of a roof. On the left side, have a buddy hold one piece of lath on the face of the play-house wherever you find a solid spot to drive a screw. Drive a screw through the lath and into the wall. Repeat this on the right side. With the help of a buddy, lean the two pieces inward until they cross, with about a 4" overhang on each top. Predrill a hole where the two boards cross with a ⅛" drill bit, and then drive your screw through both boards. If you choose not to predrill, the wood will probably crack a little bit, which is why you leave at least 4" of overhang. Repeat this step on the back.

13. Get your pals and climb into your house. Let the fun begin!

ASHLEY

AGE: **16**
LOCATION: **Colorado Springs, Colorado**
WHERE ASHLEY LEARNS: **The MiLL**

SkillsUSA®
STATE
CHAMPION
CABINETMAKING
2019

> *My favorite part of building it was spending time with my dad in the garage.*

What are some things you want us to know about you?

I've been building at the MiLL for three years now, and before that I built as a side hobby with my dad. I've played soccer for ten years. I've also been in orchestra, playing the violin, for six years. I hunt large game and small game, and I got my first buck this last hunting season. I like to camp with my family. I have an older sister who is a freshman in college, studying to be a nurse, and a younger sister who is a sophomore in high school. I am number one in cabinet manufacturing in the state of Colorado for SkillsUSA. It was a big shock to me because I didn't really expect to get first. When they said my name I was really proud of myself. When I finished early I went through and fixed little mistakes and sanded while there was still time.

What is the first thing you ever built?

The first big thing I remember building is my bed frame. It's like 3' tall and made of aspen and, I think, maple. I built it because my old bed frame broke and I was sleeping on my mattress on the ground, so my dad decided that we would build a new bed frame for me. I was thirteen or fourteen years old. My favorite part of building it was spending time with my dad in the garage.

How does building make you feel?

It makes me feel like I can do a lot of things that people say girls normally can't do. This is typically a "man's world," and it makes me feel accomplished when I can do something as well as or better than most boys. And it's a good stress relief to get out and put stuff together.

Why do you build?

I guess I just always saw my dad building and always wanted to be like my dad. It kind of grew on me. Right now I'm doing it for fun. My favorite tool is the table saw because it can do so many things, like it can cut boards down and prepare different joints. With the right add-ons, it can do angled cuts.

What advice do you have for other girls?

My advice would be to go for it even if other people say or think that you can't. You can pretty much do anything you set your mind to.

What's the first step in trying something new?

Sign up for a class. That way you don't have to get too far into the commitment but you get to try it out for little to no cost.

Who do you look up to?

I look up to my mom and my dad the most because they've taught me how to be a good person and how to persevere. They're just really big role models in my life. Whenever I would fail at something, they would teach me how to get better; when I would make a mistake, they wouldn't get mad at me. They would calm me down and teach me how to do it better.

What are some other activities that make you feel courageous, strong, and bold?

I think soccer does because soccer is a contact sport. When you get pushed around you have to get back up again. You don't win all the games and you don't lose all the games, and when you win you are grateful, and you learn from the losses.

What are some ideas of things girls can build at home?

It can be as small as a birdhouse or small table. If you have a lathe you can make things like bowls and pens.

What project are you sharing with us?

It's an heirloom tool chest. It has six drawers and it's going to have a lid. The legs are made from poplar and it has multiple mortise and tenon joints that we are cutting by hand. It's going to be sturdy and never come apart.

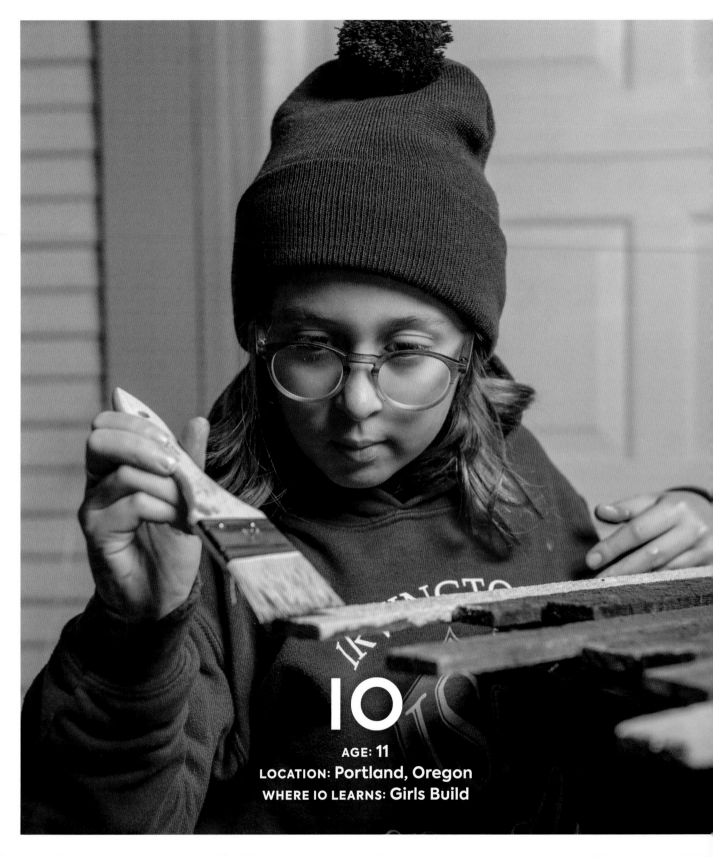

IO

AGE: 11
LOCATION: Portland, Oregon
WHERE IO LEARNS: Girls Build

> *Building makes me feel strong,*
> *big, powerful, and important.*

What are some things you want us to know about you?

My dad and my baba (my mom's dad) both build things, and I have built things with them. I play trumpet, and I love to do art.

What is the first thing you ever built?

The first real building thing I remember making is a teddy bear picnic table with Baba. But the first small thing was sanding and painting designs on a wooden salmon that my dad cut out for a preschool class project (I think I was three and a half).

How does building make you feel?

Building makes me feel strong, big, powerful, and important.

Why do you build?

Because it has a satisfying outcome. I like the feeling of having to work hard and having something to show for it, something cool or useful or just satisfying.

What advice would you give to other girls?

It often takes teamwork, and don't be afraid to ask for help. Because building things can be hard, and takes time. Also, always persevere. It's worth it!

What is the first step in trying something new?

For me, the mindset. Perseverance!

Who do you look up to?

In the building world it is Katie Hughes! Because she is a woman and is strong and builds cool things. I think it is always awesome to see a woman doing things that are not stereotypically a "woman's job," because that makes me feel strong, powerful, and hopeful that I can do things like that too.

Beyond the building world I look up to the musician and singer Lizzo because she is a strong black woman who has gotten far by being herself and using her talents. I like her mindset and messages about just being yourself. Even if other people aren't feeling you, you feel you. She thinks that's important. I do too!

What other activities make you feel courageous, strong, and bold?

I feel courageous, bold, and strong when I am doing sports like soccer and basketball, and sometimes in mathematics because I know math is hard and useful. Math people are often men, so I like being good at something that generally girls aren't told to be good at.

What are some ideas of things girls can build at home?

Anything with Popsicle sticks! I recommend making structures out of things from the recycling bin because they are easy to make, and you have easy access to materials without help. You can cut, glue, and create all sorts of stuff with tools that you already have. And you can make things as cool or advanced as you want!

What project are you sharing with us?

A picture frame out of lath—another recycled item!

REBA

AGE: 14
LOCATION: Portland, Oregon
WHERE REBA LEARNS: Girls Build

> *No matter how much you struggle, the more you let things go, the faster it will become the past.*

What are some things you want us to know about you?

I live with my grandma and my sister, and we live at Bridge Meadows, which is a place where foster kids can hang out. We have a nice backyard and stuff. My sister and I went into foster care when I was around seven—it was about to be my birthday. I went with my foster family for, like, three months, and then my grandma took us in. We are still friends with our foster family, and we act like sisters. Soul sisters, maybe? Anyway, my grandma adopted us when I was about ten. My dad still visits us, and our mom sometimes, too.

When I grow up I hope to do something with birds and animals, because I really like animals. I like to draw animals—I am really bad at drawing humans but I try. Sometimes I draw creatures I make up in my mind, and a lot of cats. I go to Da Vinci, which is an arts school. I like it, but they don't have PE, which is a bummer because I really like PE and sports. I would like to take more hikes—sometimes we go to Audubon [a wildlife sanctuary] and OMSI [Oregon Museum of Science and Industry] for camps. I would like to do more bird hikes outside of camp, because I would like to study birds more. You can't study them much just outside your house.

What is the first thing you ever built?

I think it was the clocks at Girls Build camp. They were really fun. I had a lot of fun sanding them. I found out that I really enjoy sanding things. That clock is on the wall of my room right now.

How does building make you feel?

It makes me feel strong and hopeful about girl power. Having all this stuff in my room reminds me that girls and women can do anything they want, no matter who they are or how people see or label them.

Why do you build?

I build because of the memories I create at camp, with my friends and the counselors there. I like the mood of really building— not like DIY stuff, but doing challenging things like we can't do at other camps. We can use saws and power tools, and it's really cool. When you need help, people can help each other, and it creates a bond. The counselors have a really great bond together, and I like watching them laugh together.

What advice do you have for other girls?

Don't worry about things too much. You will get through it. You can do it. No matter how much you struggle, the more you let things go, the faster it will become the past.

What's the first step in trying something new?

Think about how people start. If you make a mistake, don't beat yourself up. Don't be afraid to do anything new, especially if you are with professionals. They have tried something new, made mistakes, and failed. Failing makes you learn from your mistakes faster. Whatever it is might be your new career when you grow up.

Who do you look up to?

I never really looked up to anyone. Technically everyone has helped me through my life—teachers, counselors, guardians, counselors at camp. They have all helped me become a better person.

What are some other activities that make you feel courageous, strong, and bold?

Bird-watching! Bird-watching with people is really fun. Identifying every bird I see, and knowing that I'm really good at bird-watching. I love teaching people about what birds live where, bird behavior, different birdcalls. I feel really proud because there aren't a lot of things I am extremely good at, and I just enjoy being in the natural world.

What are some ideas of things girls can build at home?

Maybe if the screws come out of the door, you can fix it. People will say, "Oh my gosh, you are so cool." A table, because that would be really cool. Technically, anything you put your mind to.

What project are you sharing with us?

A shelf made from an old drawer.

REBA'S SALVAGED SHELF

Reba decided to build a shelf out of a used drawer, turning it on its side and adding some shelving. We built this in the wood shop of the ReBuilding Center, a warehouse that sells salvaged (reusable) building goods. (Look for a Habitat for Humanity ReStore in your area for something similar.) Reba was able to do some browsing, and she chose a drawer and shelving materials that she liked. Reba had a blast, laughing a lot and rolling her eyes for the camera in the best way possible. Her bubbliness is infectious, and everyone had a great time documenting this build. Since this project uses salvaged materials, we can't call out the specific measurements, but we will guide you through the process. This is a simple shelf, fun to make, and cute to hang up!

MATERIALS

- ❏ Wooden drawer, size of your choosing
- ❏ ¾" shelf material (¾" refers to the thickness of the wood). See step 1 to determine how much wood you need. Most shelves are 3" deep, so you can get 1x3 boards that may fit, or rip (cut) down longer boards on a table saw (a skilled adult should do this for you). (Remember, boards that are called 1x are actually only ¾" thick. Check out the Materials Glossary for more information. The Glossary is fun, I promise!)
- ❏ 1½" screws, 4 per shelf

- ❏ Optional: Reba added little hooks and nails to the bottom of her shelf to hang items like keys. Feel free to gather similar items to attach to the bottom of your shelf.

TOOLS

- ❏ Tape measure
- ❏ Pencil
- ❏ Speed square
- ❏ Jigsaw or chop saw
- ❏ Finish hammer
- ❏ Drill
- ❏ Drill bits to match screws
- ❏ 2 bar clamps
- ❏ ⅛" bit
- ❏ ¹⁄₁₆" bit

Adult oversight:

Cost after tools:

Safety gear:
- Safety glasses
- Ear protection

Work surface:
Flat and sturdy bench or table

Skill level:

Time:

STEPS

1. Put on safety glasses and ear protection. Check for and remove loose clothing and jewelry, and make sure hair is tied back.

2. You'll need to figure out how much shelf material you need. Reba's drawer is almost 12" wide. She wants three shelves, so she needs 3' of wood for her shelves. To figure out how much you need, measure across your drawer. Multiply that number by the number of shelves you would like, and that's how much shelf material you need. 12" x 3 = 36". So, 36" is 3'.

3. Let's talk about the drawer real quick. The part of the drawer that is the front will now become the top of your shelf. The back of the drawer is now the bottom.

4. The first measurement you need is inside your drawer, from the inside left to the inside right. Get the correct measurement by bumping the metal end of the tape into the side on the left, then stretching the tape across the right, over the top of the wood. Look to see where the wood on the inside right meets the tape measure—that's your measurement. If you are left-handed, run the tape measure from right to left.

5. Write this number down somewhere so you can come back to it. Now, gather your shelving material. Measure out your first shelf, using the measurement you just figured out. Mark it with a crow's foot, then draw a line through the crow's foot with your speed square (see page 30 for instructions on making a crow's foot).

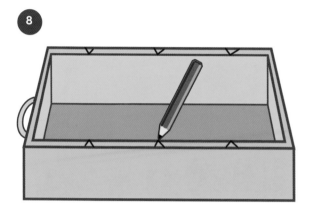

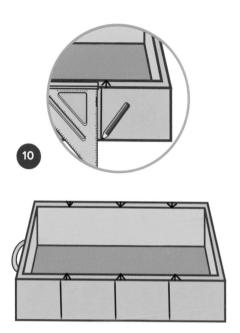

- -

6. Using safe cutting practices, either clamp your wood to your work surface with the cut line hanging over the edge and cut it with the jigsaw, or use the chop saw to cut it (see page 41 for instructions on using these saws).

7. Repeat steps 4 and 5 for as many shelves as you need.

8. Next, you need to figure out where your shelves will go. Again, this is your decision. (If you want equal space between your shelves, measure the length of your drawer, then divide it by the number of shelves you want plus one.) Reba has three shelves, so she would divide the length of her drawer by four. Once decided, mark your measurements on the face of the drawer where you want the bottom of each

shelf with crow's feet. Make sure to mark both sides of the drawer. Draw a straight line through your crow's foot with your speed square.

9. You need to draw center lines to screw through. Take your tape measure and measure ⅜" below the crow's foot that is currently there. You may need to burn 1" or 2" to get this precise measurement. Make a crow's foot and then, hooking your speed square on the line, draw a line down the outside of your drawer. Repeat this on each crow's foot.

10. Pick up a shelf piece, and slide it into its spot in the drawer, lining up the bottom of your shelf with the crow's foot on the face of the drawer. If the shelf feels tight, you can use your hammer to gently tap the shelf into place,

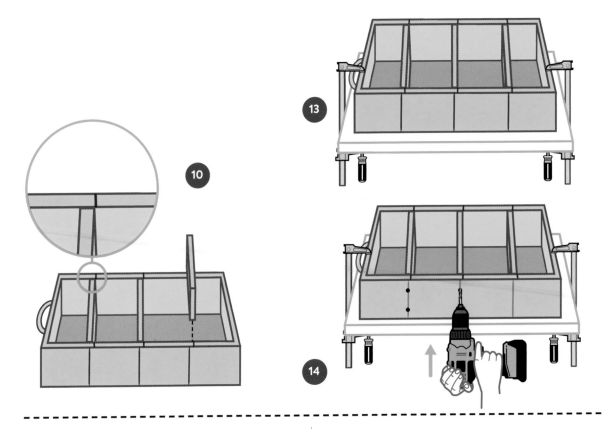

making sure not to scratch the wood. Insert all shelves.

11. Reba liked the look of having her shelf sit on screws on the inside, while she used a nail gun on the outside. We are going to skip the internal screws and just drive screws through the outside of the drawer into the shelf.

12. Turn the drawer so your shelves are perpendicular to the edge of your work surface. Bring the drawer close to the edge of your work surface. If your shelves are nicely lined up with your marks on the inside of your drawer, get your drill ready. Start with the ⅛" bit.

13. You can now clamp your drawer to the work surface to provide extra support, or have a buddy hold it steady on the work surface.

14. After double-checking that the center of your shelves line up with the center lines on the outside of the drawer, drill two holes into each line you drew on the outside of the drawer, roughly 2" apart and 1" from the top or bottom edge of the drawer (again, roughly). If your drawer is deeper than Reba's, you can spread your screws farther apart. Try to stay about 1" from each edge in order to avoid splitting the wood, and make sure you still are boring holes into the lines you drew.

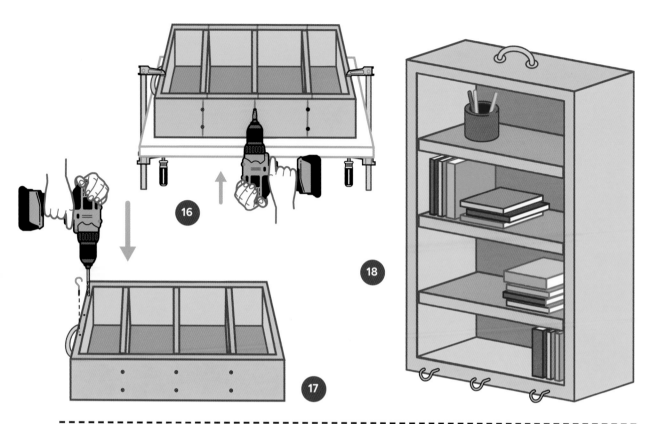

15. Once the holes are drilled, drive one screw into each pilot hole and into the shelves, securing the shelves.

16. Once each shelf is secured into your drawer, it's time to add hooks underneath, if you choose this option. You might need to predrill some holes to secure your hooks. The idea is to have them hang below your shelf if it is hanging on a wall. Choose the location for each hook, predrill with a ¹⁄₁₆″ bit, and screw the hooks in.

17. Once your shelf unit is complete, you can hang it by screwing directly through the back into the wall. (You'll need an adult to help you drill into studs. If you can't find studs—it's hard!—use drywall anchors.) Place your screw right at the top of your drawer. It's likely that there is a gap between the back of your drawer and the wall. That's okay! Just don't drive your screw all the way through the back.

18. Fill your shelf with things you love!

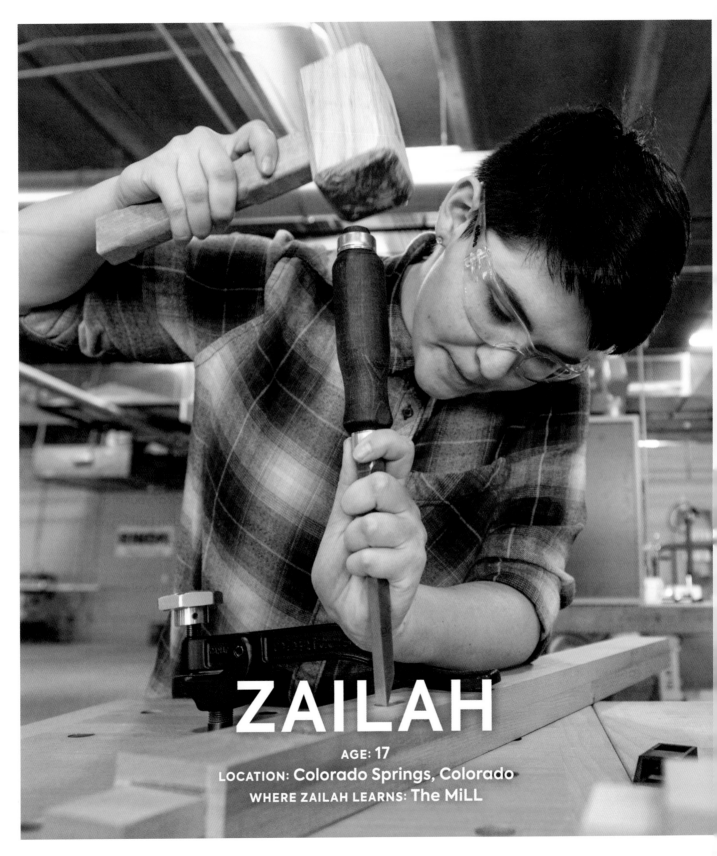

ZAILAH

AGE: 17
LOCATION: Colorado Springs, Colorado
WHERE ZAILAH LEARNS: The MiLL

> *Everyone's going to be nervous trying something new, but it's worth trying at least once.*

What are some things you want us to know about you?

I was five when I first started working on cars. My dad thought it was a good thing to learn at a young age, or having it for the future. Even something as simple as an oil change can save you money. I also like to do photography. In the summer and fall I do marching band. I am also in the color guard line. I do winter guard too, which is a bunch of people on a gym floor with flags. I have seven siblings, and I am in the middle. My big thing with my dad is that he wanted to do adoption, so three of my siblings are adopted.

What is the first thing you ever built?

When I was twelve I did a restore job with my uncle because he was into cars. We rebuilt an entire 1967 Mustang. That was one of my best jobs—we had to completely restore the body, the interior, the engine, everything. That was my proudest work.

How does building make you feel?

Building for me is a sense of relaxing. I can forget about the world around me and I can just put all my efforts into one work or project. Once you realize that you are halfway done, you are like, wow, I didn't realize the time, because you are so busy working on it.

Why do you build?

I build sometimes for myself, and sometimes for others. I like seeing someone's reaction to how good the work is. It makes me feel, like, a sense of awe that, dang, I brought someone happiness because it looks good.

What advice do you have for other girls?

Don't let someone dictate what you can or can't do. In the future you can prove them wrong. If someone is bullying you, you can show them that you are the better person, that it doesn't get to you. If you say that I'm not good enough, then I'm going to do these things you say I can't do.

What's the first step in trying something new?

The first step in trying something new is stepping outside of your comfort zone. People get in a sense of repetition while going about their day. You can take small steps into what you want to do. Or just go and do it, if you can. Everyone's going to be nervous trying something new, but it's worth trying at least once. Try not to let it hold you back that you're nervous.

Who do you look up to?

It's kind of hard to say. I don't really have a model to look up to. My parents weren't home when I was younger, and my older siblings—we fight a lot. There's no one that I've had a chance to look up to for something like that. My dad worked a road job, and my mom took a second job to make ends meet. I mean, eight kids.

What are some other activities that make you feel courageous, strong, and bold?

I used to do mixed martial arts. I'm trained in four areas of fighting. It was definitely something that made me feel strong. A lot of people called me courageous because taking punches to the face is something some people just don't want. I think it's definitely a brave sport.

What are some ideas of things girls can build at home?

You can easily build a little placard for your name, or you can build a name plate— they're pretty simple pieces to do with a piece of wood and paint or a carving knife.

What project are you sharing with us?

The base for a tool chest.

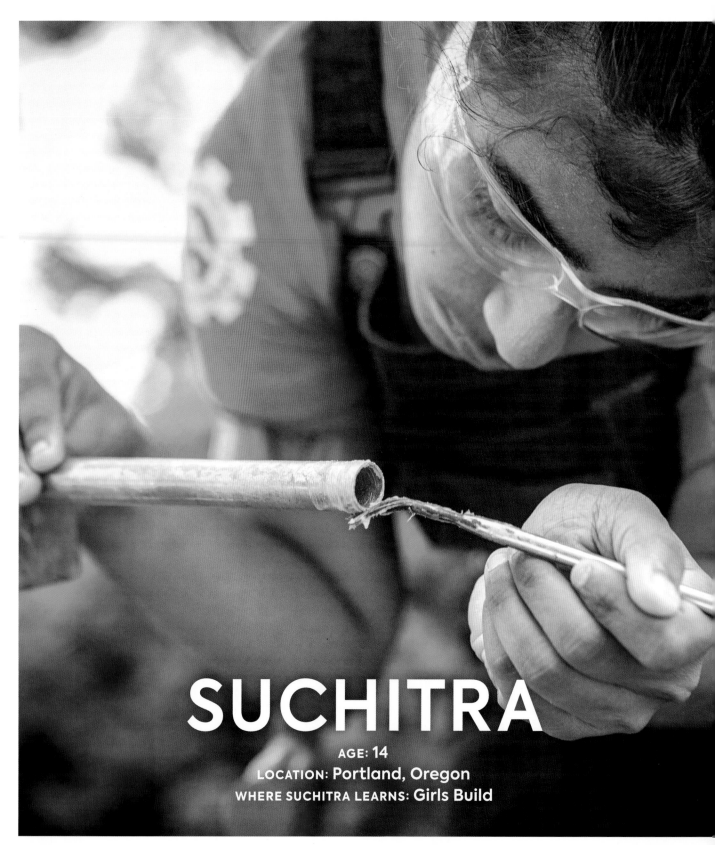

SUCHITRA

AGE: **14**
LOCATION: **Portland, Oregon**
WHERE SUCHITRA LEARNS: **Girls Build**

> *Be courageous and bold with your ideas.*

What are some things you want us to know about you?
I have dyslexia, ADHD, and cerebral palsy. I love musicals, movies, and *Murder, She Wrote*. I am adopted from India. I play wheelchair basketball and tennis. I love being with my family and friends.

What is the first thing you ever built?
I built bookshelves with my grandpa.

How does building make you feel?
It makes me feel excited.

Why do you build?
I build because I enjoy working with my hands and tools. I also feel happy to work with other people.

What advice do you have for other girls?
Be courageous and bold with your ideas. Be yourself, and people will like you for who you are.

What's the first step in trying something new?
Taking new chances and being yourself the whole way through.

Who do you look up to?
I look up to my mom because she helps people every day with housing.

What other activities make you feel courageous, bold, and strong?
Wheelchair basketball, acting, and swimming.

What are some ideas of things girls can build at home?
A tree house, playhouses, and raised beds to put veggies in.

What project are you sharing with us?
A lamp with a wooden base and copper arm that I made at camp.

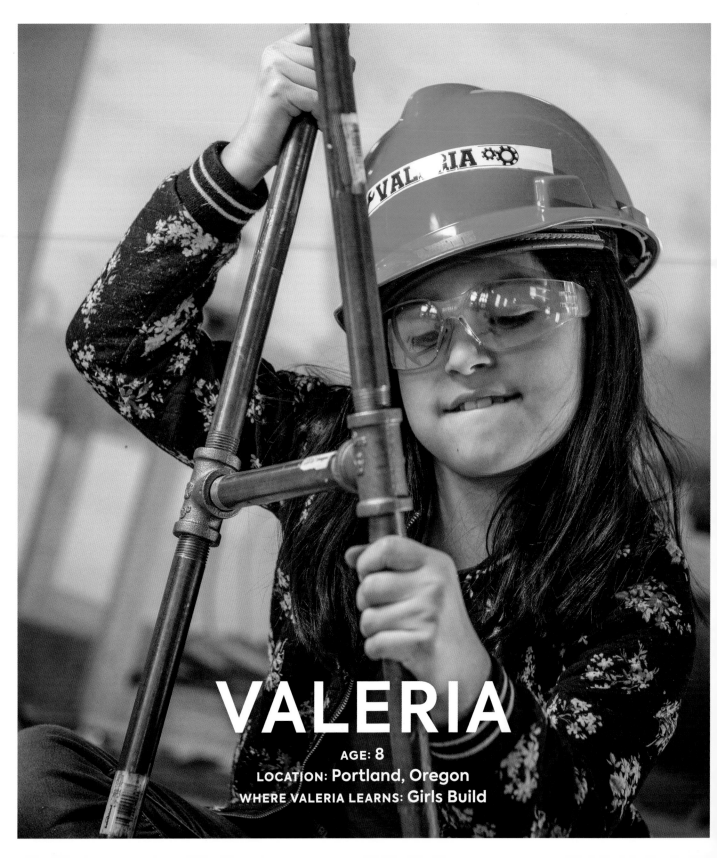

VALERIA

AGE: **8**
LOCATION: **Portland, Oregon**
WHERE VALERIA LEARNS: **Girls Build**

> *Sometimes people don't let girls build,*
> *and so I am happy that there is*
> *a place where I get to build.*

What are some things you want us to know about you?

I have a dog and a cat, and I love to build. I have built a lot of things, like a noisemaker and masks, but nothing too big.

What is the first thing you ever built?

The first thing I ever built was a noisemaker out of a toilet paper tube.

How does building make you feel?

Adventurous. And also if I want something and I make it, I feel proud of myself.

Why do you build?

Because I like building. I love it! Sometimes people don't let girls build, and so I am happy that there is a place where I get to build.

What advice would you give to other girls?

When you are using a hammer, don't swing it; just lightly hammer your nail, because you or someone else can get hurt if you swing it.

What's the first step in trying something new?

Believe in yourself and don't start right away; you have to take baby steps because you don't know everything. You need to find someone who can help you do it and who knows how to do it. Do it with them, and then do it by yourself.

Who do you look up to?

I look up to a lot of people; some of them are my teachers because I want to learn and know how to have fun and make a lot of friends.

What other activities make you feel courageous, bold, and strong?

I like singing and I like dancing. I like playing instruments, and sometimes I just like to relax. Also going on adventures.

What are some ideas of things girls can build at home?

Well, you could build a birdhouse, you could build tiny wooden dolls, or you could build a little teepee. You could make a little dollhouse, and you could make masks. And you can make a lamp, but for that you would need help from a grown-up. There's a lot of things you can build at home, not just in other places.

What project are you sharing with us?

I built a nightstand out of pipes and wood.

VALERIA'S NIGHTSTAND

Valeria made her nightstand on the floor of a friend's barn. She was excited to use the big pipes and get her hands a little greasy. She took many breaks to get cheesy for the camera, and she had a ton of fun. This kid is outgoing, fun, and excited. And she loves her new nightstand.

MATERIALS

The following are all ½" black gas-pipe fittings:

- ❏ Six 6" nipples (pieces of pipe)
- ❏ 6 caps
- ❏ 8 tees
- ❏ Five 10" nipples
- ❏ Four 8" nipples
- ❏ 4 floor flanges
- ❏ Two 90-degree elbows (Double-check that you don't get street elbows.)
- ❏ 4 close nipples (This just means that they are very small and are essentially completely threaded.)
- ❏ ¾" plywood that measures at least 16" x 16" (You can often buy precut plywood that measures 24" x 24" at big-box lumber stores. This is for your tabletop, so choose wisely.)
- ❏ 16 ¾" screws, with wide, flat, countersunk heads (Look for a package that says #10 x ¾" flathead Phillips. You need a very wide head so it doesn't slide through the holes in the flanges.)

TOOLS

- ❏ 2 pipe wrenches
- ❏ Jigsaw
- ❏ Sander
- ❏ 80 grit and 120 grit sandpaper
- ❏ Pencil
- ❏ One more pencil or a black permanent marker
- ❏ Tape measure
- ❏ Speed square and ruler
- ❏ "Clean for wood" jigsaw blade
- ❏ Drill with bit that matches your screws
- ❏ 15" of string
- ❏ #3 Phillips bit
- ❏ ⅛" drill bit

SKILLS

- ❏ Measuring
- ❏ Drilling
- ❏ Using a pipe wrench
- ❏ Sawing

Adult oversight:

Cost after tools:

Safety gear:
- Safety glasses
- Fitted gloves (if you want to avoid greasy hands)

Work surface: Flat, stable floor or table

Skill level:

Time:

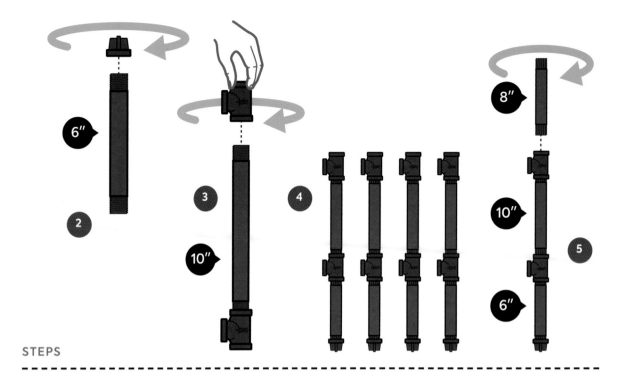

STEPS

1. Put on safety glasses and gloves. Check for and remove loose clothing and jewelry, and make sure hair is tied back. These pipes are very greasy, and your hands will be covered in grease by the time you are finished. You've been warned!

2. Begin by taking four of the 6″ nipples and screwing a cap onto one end of each one. Turn either piece until it's as tight as you can make it.

3. Next, get out eight tees and four 10″ nipples. Attach one tee to each end of each 10″ nipple by screwing them on.

4. Pick up one of your capped 6″ pipes from step 2. Connect this piece to a 10″ pipe by screwing the open end into one of the 10″ pipe's tees, so you have four long pieces starting with a capped 6″ piece and ending with a tee.

5. On each of the four pieces, screw an 8″ nipple into the tee on the opposite end from the 6″ nipple.

6. Take a minute to tighten all your joints by hand and then with your pipe wrench. These are the legs of your nightstand, which might require adjusting. Once tightened, measure each leg and adjust until the legs are all the same length.

7. On one of the legs, screw another 6″ nipple into the bottom tee (the one that is connected to the capped 6″ piece). We will call this the "perpendicular 6″ nipple." Repeat with one more leg and 6″ nipple.

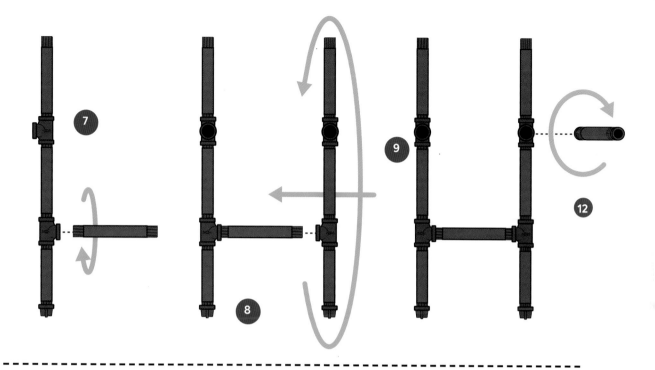

8. Take one of the two remaining legs (*without the perpendicular 6″ nipple*), and screw it to one of the legs *with* the perpendicular 6″ nipple. You will attach it at the open tee that corresponds to it (the tee attached to the perpendicular 6″ nipple). This will require a lot of big rotations of one pipe as you twist it.

9. Keep turning and turning until the two joined legs look like an H. Assemble the remaining two legs and 6″ nipples so you have two H's.

10. Now tighten all your connections with a pipe wrench. Keep making small adjustments so that when you are done, all the open tees face up—that is, perpendicular to the short bar of the H.

11. Now is the time to really tighten every joint. Make sure you don't just tighten the pipes themselves, but get your wrench or wrenches on the actual joints and spin them. If your joints are not tight, the next step will be frustrating. Plus, this is your last chance to tighten, so really go get it.

12. Screw the remaining 10″ nipple into one of the open ports on one of the H pieces.

13. You are now going to attach one H to the other via the 10″ nipple you added in step 12. You want to attach it via the opposite tee. So, if you inserted the 10″ nipple into the *right* tee on one H, attach it to the other H via the *left* tee. To do this, lift the entire second H, set it on the 10″ nipple of the first H, and spin the entire

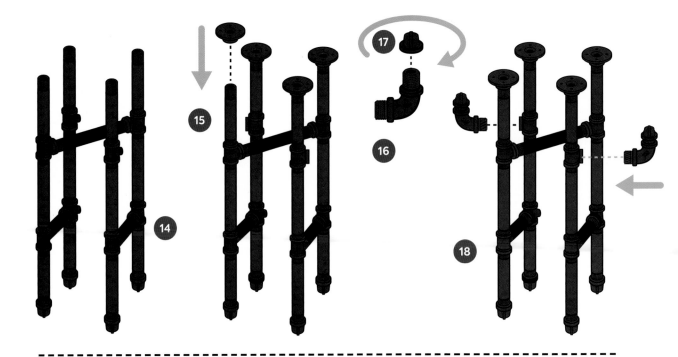

second H around in a huge circle. Make this as tight as you can—really wrestle with it—and stop turning when it is very tight and each H is a mirror image of the other.

14. When you are done tightening, your table might not look like a table at all. The 10" nipple should run diagonally between the H legs. Adjust the angles until the whole project looks more like a set of table legs. Set it on its feet (the caps).

15. Screw a flange onto the open end at the top of each leg.

16. Into the two open tees, you are going to install little hooks for your headphones or whatever else you might want to hang there. Get the two elbows, four close nipples, and two

remaining caps. Into each elbow, screw in two close nipples as tight as you can with your hand.

17. Onto one of the elbows, hand tighten a cap. Repeat with the other elbow.

18. Screw one elbow into an open port on one of the open tees on the legs. Repeat on the other open port. The hooks are complete! You can make these hooks face whichever way you'd like—facing in, facing out, facing off to the side. You decide. Adjust them by using the pipe wrench.

19. Get out the board you are going to use as the top. You can make the size whatever you want, but for ours, the top is 16" x 16". Measure from one edge of the board to 16", then make a crow's foot. Keeping your tape measure hooked

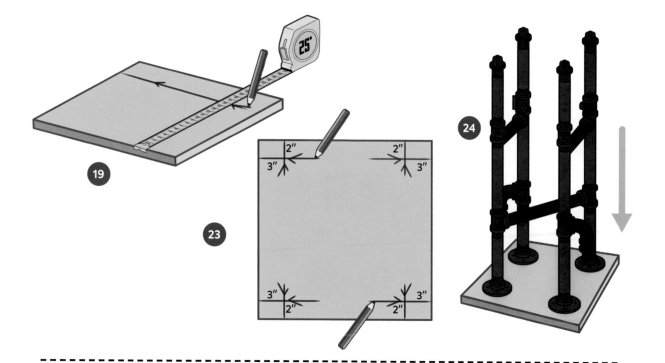

on that same side, slide the tape measure down the board and make another mark at 16". This will create two points between which you can draw a line.

20. Connect the two crow's feet by drawing a line using a piece of wood or a ruler as a straightedge. Repeat step 19, drawing a line perpendicular to the line you just drew.

21. Cut along your line using the jigsaw (or, if you are a very well-trained adult, the table saw, sliding chop saw, or circular saw).

22. You should now have a square that will be your tabletop. Decide which side will be the top (it should be the better-looking and smoother side). Set it on the ground or on a flat surface in a clean area with the top facing down.

23. Measure 3" from any edge. Use your speed square to draw a line. On the same edge but on the other end, repeat this measurement and line. Perpendicular to each of these lines, measure out 2" and draw a line through that measurement. You should have two lines that cross each other. Turn your wood so that those marks are on the left side. Now, repeat those measurements on the right side, beginning by pulling a 3" measurement from the right edge.

24. Get the legs, and set them upside down near the center of the square board, with the flanges facing down.

25. It's time to make the legs square (see Glossary). I did some math (thanks, Pythagoras!), and the distance between the legs that aren't attached by the 10" nipple

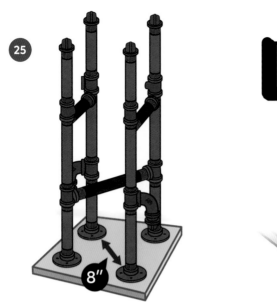

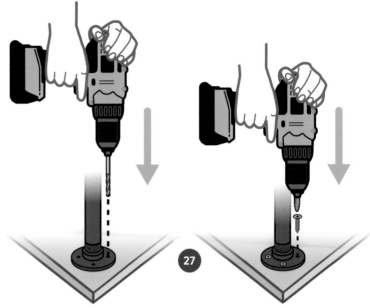

---

should be 8". Adjust them, pushing the H pieces toward each other or pulling them apart, until there is 8" *between* the legs, not outside to outside.

26. Each flange should sit inside the line you drew in step 23. If they don't fit easily, try turning the whole base 45 degrees. After you fiddle with the legs, adjust the flanges so that all four legs are sitting nicely on the flat surface of the tabletop without wobbling. For Valeria's table, this meant tightening one flange with a pipe wrench, and loosening another. This might get frustrating—stick with it.

27. Next, predrill the holes to accept the screws. Place the ⅛" bit into your drill. Bore a very short hole (remember, your board is only ¾" thick and you don't want your drill bit to

go all the way through) into an existing screw opening in one of the flanges. For the best stability, bore one hole, drive a screw, then bore the remaining three holes. This will prevent the flange from slipping while you drill holes.

28. Repeat this process on each flange, boring holes and drilling screws, until every hole has a screw in it. Congratulations! Your table is complete!

29. P.S. If you want to keep going, here's something else you can do. I cut the top of this nightstand into a circle because I thought it would be cute. Here's how to do that. Turn your table right-side up. Find the center by measuring 8" from two perpendicular edges and making a mark where they meet.

30. Once you have your center marked, get a string (at least 15" long) and a pencil. A round pencil is preferred in this scenario. Tie the string to the pencil, lay your pencil down flat, then pull the string out to about 10" or 12" from the edge of your pencil. Use another pencil or a marker to mark the string at 8"—make a nice dark mark, but make sure it's not too wide.

31. Press the marked spot of your string onto the center mark (8") of your tabletop. Lower the knot in the string to the lowest point of the pencil while not letting the string slide off. This should be near where you are holding the pencil.

32. With one hand holding the string on your center mark, use your other hand to slowly draw a circle around your center mark, keeping your pencil nice and straight. Double-check every so often that your marked point on your string does not move off the center point of the tabletop.

33. Once your circle is drawn, get out your jigsaw. Following your line closely, cut out a circle. Your cut should be close to the edge of your board.

34. You may also want to sand down your top. Additionally, you may stain or paint the tabletop.

35. Okay, now your table is truly finished! And it's so cute with that round top! One tip: If the legs are wobbly, you can adjust them by tightening or loosening the caps on the bottoms of the legs.

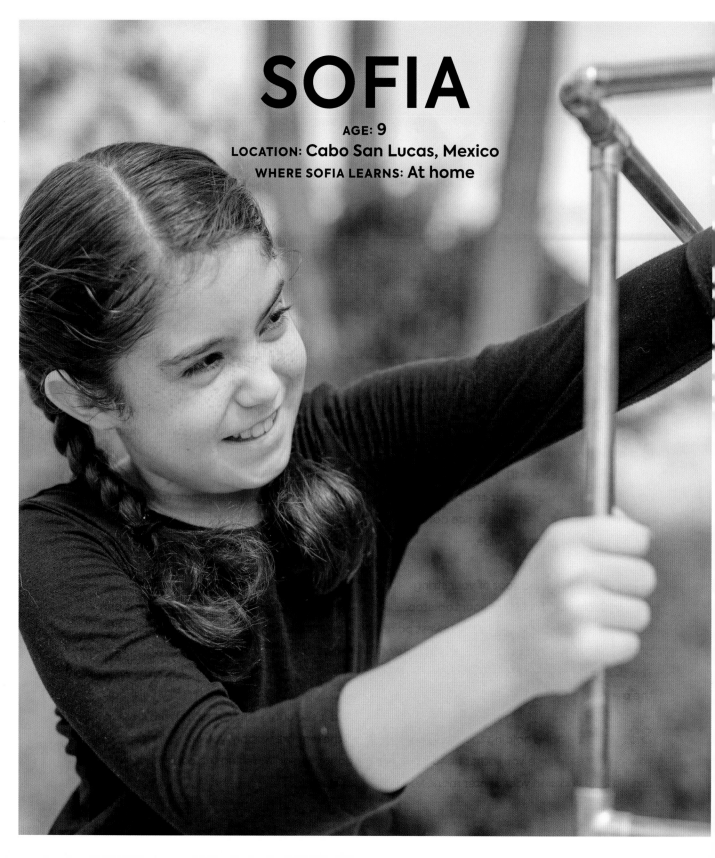

SOFIA

AGE: 9
LOCATION: Cabo San Lucas, Mexico
WHERE SOFIA LEARNS: At home

Believe in yourself because you can do anything!

What are some things you want us to know about you?
I love animals, especially horses.

What is the first thing you ever built?
A Popsicle house and jellyfish, origami birds, newspaper hearts.

How does building make you feel?
Proud of myself.

Why do you build?
Because it's fun!

What advice do you have for other girls?
Believe in yourself because you can do anything! Don't give up, and keep trying.

Who do you look up to?
My mom because she knows lots of things.

What other activities make you feel courageous, strong, and bold?
Swimming, working with tools, and accomplishing something.

What are some ideas of things girls can build at home?
Birdhouses, birdbaths, bat boxes, and mailboxes.

What project are you sharing with us?
A copper stool that I cut the pieces for and soldered together. I love it!

NyASIA

AGE: 11
LOCATION: Manchester, New Hampshire
WHERE NyASIA LEARNS: Girls at Work

> *Just because it looks hard doesn't mean you can't try or succeed.*

What are some things you want us to know about you?

I am funny. I like to laugh a lot. I like trying new things, and last but not least, I love love love my family.

What is the first thing you ever built?

In fifth grade we had to make a miniature playground for kids with disabilities because we thought it was unfair that some people can't do the basics on a playground like other people can.

How does building make you feel?

Building makes me feel happy and unstoppable because I never thought I could build. But if I just think and focus, I can.

Why do you build?

I build because it makes me feel powerful and proud.

What advice do you have for other girls?

Just because it looks hard doesn't mean you can't try or succeed.

What's the first step in trying something new?

The first step is that you actually have to want to do it.

Who do you look up to?

I look up to my mom because she is always there for me and she never gives up.

What are some other activities that make you feel courageous, strong, and bold?

Dance, basketball, and running cross-country.

What are some ideas of things girls can build at home?

A box or shelf for the wall.

What project are you sharing with us?

My big bench that has storage inside.

LANEY

AGE: 7
LOCATION: Colorado Springs, Colorado
WHERE LANEY LEARNS: The Twine Lab

> *I think that other girls should really not be afraid of being themselves.*

What are some things you want us to know about you?

I play soccer, and I love photography. I have one older brother, and he's three years older than me. My favorite colors are green and red. My favorite food is pasta with my mom's spaghetti sauce. It has tomatoes in it and I really like tomatoes. I like to go camping, play survivor games, do Bear Grylls challenges. I am awesome.

What is the first thing you ever built?

A God's eye in art class. We also made these catapults. We got Popsicle sticks, and we got rubber bands, and we tied them in a certain way. We got a bottle cap or an egg and put it in the catapult and tried to launch it. It was during Halloween, and we used pumpkin candies and tried to launch them into people's mouths. That was probably one of the first things I ever built.

Also, my mom buys huge cans of pretzels, and I used to be able to fit into them, and we would turn them into rocket ships and my brother would push me around.

How does building make you feel?

Happy! Smart. I mainly like using all the tools. I find what I think I know how to use, and I go BOOM, and it turns into something. I like being independent because I don't get told what to do, and I get told what to do a lot at home because I'm the baby. I like working independently because I get to use tools and my own ideas.

Why do you build?

I build because it's fun and interesting. You can make, like, whatever you want sometimes.

What advice do you have for other girls?

Be you. And if you're a tomboy don't let people make fun of you. Be brave. Stand up for other people. Don't let people boss you around, saying you can't do flips or you can't do this or that. I think that other girls should really not be afraid of being themselves. I bet you could build. It's not that hard for me, and if you get stuck on it, I can help you.

What's the first step in trying something new?

Ask for help if you get stuck on something. Don't be afraid if you make mistakes—everyone makes mistakes.

Who do you look up to?

I mainly look up to my brother, Oliver, because when I was younger and I started being a tomboy, I said, "Oh, I like his hairstyle or that clothing style." I also look up to my half cousins Avery and Cora. Again, I'm the youngest, so they're always doing something new, and I try it too.

What are some other activities that make you feel courageous, strong, and bold?

Soccer and parkour. Soccer because I've been doing it for a pretty long time, since I was four years old. You get to run and sprint, and there's a lot of fun positions like goalie and forward. I mainly play goalie. I like it because I get to dive, get to jump onto the ground. I mainly stay off to the side so when a ball comes I can dive onto it.

What are some ideas of things girls can build at home?

Me and Oliver like to play Star Wars Battlefront, which is a video game. It comes with a gun, and I made one yesterday out of cardboard because we were playing Star Wars in real life. I really like cardboard because it's easy to cut. It's not like wood where you need heavy-duty saws. You usually only need scissors to cut it. You can really make everything. You just find what you have around the house.

What project are you sharing with us?

I made a book house. It's grass-green, like in the summertime. It's pretty simple to build.

AZUSA

AGE: 15
LOCATION: Richmond, California
WHERE AZUSA LEARNS: Girls Garage

> *It's an amazing feeling to step back and look at something you built . . . I want everyone to be able to experience that if they want to.*

What are some things you want us to know about you?

I'm normally an incredibly shy and antisocial person. Building, or making in general, though, has given me a confidence I can't feel anywhere else. It helps that the people at Girls Garage are so friendly and supportive, too, but I love creating and building anytime and anywhere I can.

What is the first thing you ever built?

The earliest thing I can remember building is probably a cabin-like thing made out of corks. I don't remember why I made it, but it was around Christmas, and for some reason we had gotten out a lot of corks to do something, so I took out my hot-glue gun and made a little house. It was completely spontaneous and kind of useless, but it was fun to make.

How does building make you feel?

Building makes me feel like I can do anything. Seeing something you helped create that started out as a thought is a great feeling, and especially if you've been working really hard at it. It's so rewarding to see something you did and be able to say, "I made that."

Why do you build?

I build because I want to. Not because someone told me to, or because I feel obliged to, but because it's fun. It's an amazing feeling to step back and look at something you built, especially when you know it's for a good cause, and I want everyone to be able to experience that if they want to. Building isn't for everyone, but it definitely is for me, and I build because I can take genuine delight in whatever I'm making.

What advice do you have for other girls?

Try to find something you love that you're willing to step out of your comfort zone for. If it holds, and you get better and better at whatever it is, your confidence will grow a lot, and that alone will help you so much. I also feel like I need to say that it does take time to gain confidence in yourself. If you get frustrated or annoyed at yourself for not being able to do something, it's completely normal, and it just shows that you're human. Trust yourself to get there eventually, and you will. I guarantee it.

What's the first step in trying something new?

The first step for me is to commit yourself to it. If you're trying something that you're not that interested in, chances are it's not going to work out. If you have something you're really invested in and want to do, try to focus on what you love about it, and it'll get easier once you take that first step.

What are some ideas of things girls can build at home?

In my opinion, the best mediums are hot glue and a bag of balsa wood. You can make houses, ships, furniture, really anything you want. I've spent countless hours on the floor of my room building random structures just because I felt like making something. Everything you create doesn't have to be practical or even make sense, but if you have fun making it, it's definitely worthwhile.

What project are you sharing with us?

The project I presented was a toolbox I made when I first started Girls Garage.

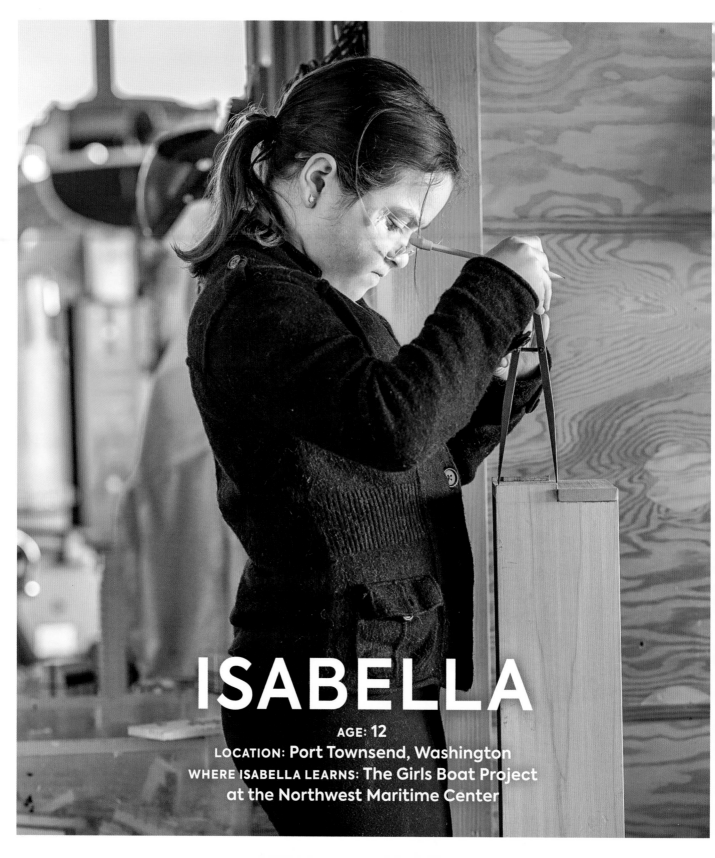

ISABELLA

AGE: **12**
LOCATION: **Port Townsend, Washington**
WHERE ISABELLA LEARNS: **The Girls Boat Project
at the Northwest Maritime Center**

> ## *If you want to learn something new, saying you can't do it is not going to get you anywhere.*

What are some things you want us to know about you?

I was born here in Port Townsend. I have an older sister named Amelia. She is fifteen. We sometimes get along, sometimes not. My favorite subjects are math and art. The Wearable Art Show happens in May. There is a student division—it is clothing that is not necessarily art, something that you could wear every day but that an artist made. This year I am making a kimono out of butter boxes, and I will be Madame Butterfly.

I like to read and clean my room. I like it to be nice and tidy. Sometimes I think it's a bad habit because I do it constantly, but sometimes it just happens to be messy because I am doing a project or rearranging my room. So I have to tell myself it's okay to be messy. I usually wear cat ears every day, but I don't wear them in the shop. I also like to sew. I've always liked to make things with my hands. I like baking. It's fun to make delicious things. I like to bake everything—sweets in general.

What is the first thing you ever built?

I'm not exactly sure what the first thing I built was, but probably a wooden toy boat at the wooden boat festival when I was about four or five. I always do that.

How does building make you feel?

It makes me feel like I can do anything I want to do and no one can stop me.

Why do you build?

Because I like to. It makes me think about what size a shape is and how it will turn out, like in math, but in building you never know exactly how it will turn out. You could do something where you think it will look one way but it doesn't in the end. Sometimes I like the way it turned out, and sometimes I think, "I wanted it to be perfect!"

What advice do you have for other girls?

If you are interested in something, you should pursue it, because there are so many amazing opportunities out there. Follow what you want to do, and you will be able to do it.

What's the first step in trying something new?

I either ask for help from parents or a peer that can help me, or I find a class. If you see something that you want to do, go for it. Because it's not really good to say, "I can't do that because I don't know how." If you want to learn something new, saying you can't do it is not going to get you anywhere.

Who do you look up to?

I look up to my parents. They are awesome and help me pursue what I want to do. I also look up to my friends because they help me do what I want to do too.

What are some other activities that make you feel courageous, strong, and bold?

I like to bake. When you bake a cake, and it's good, everyone says it's so delicious. I like making people happy and giving them something they can enjoy.

What are some ideas of things girls can build at home?

Well, taking a piece of wood and drilling a hole in it, putting a stick in it, making a sail—you can make it a boat. You can use fabric or something for the sail.

What project are you sharing with us?

A tray I made last year in the Girls Boat Project.

MATERIALS GLOSSARY

BLACK GAS PIPE/BLACK PIPE

When you go to a store that carries plumbing supplies, you will see a few different types of pipe that screw together. This is what you are looking for. Some of the pieces are black, some are silver. I use the black because it looks nice, but you can use whatever makes you happy. The silver pipe is galvanized (which means it's coated in zinc), so it would be excellent to use if your final product will end up outside. Here are some of the pieces you might see:

- ½" x 12" nipple (or piece of pipe): ½" refers to the diameter, and 12" refers to the length (you will also see other lengths—for example, 6", 8", 10").
- ½" tee: ½" refers to the diameter, and "tee" refers to the shape.
- ½" cap: ½" refers to the diameter, and "cap" refers to the shape. This is a solid piece that will screw onto the end of a pipe, closing it off.
- ½" floor flange: ½" refers to the diameter of the center hole. The entire piece is larger, 3" to 4" in diameter, depending on the size you choose. It is essentially a circle with a threaded hole in the center. There will be four holes to screw the item into a piece of wood or into the floor.

BOLT

Bolts can be confused with screws. An easy way to remember the difference is that bolts have a blunt end and need a predrilled hole to slide through. A bolt also requires a nut and a washer to make a secure connection. Bolts come in many lengths, thicknesses, head shapes, and coatings, so go explore at your local hardware store with your parents or chaperones. Bolts are used when a stronger connection is needed than a screw would provide. For example, if you were building a deck and needed to put up railings so people don't fall off the deck, you would connect the posts of the railings to the deck with bolts. When buying bolts, nuts, and washers, make sure to get all the same type. For example, if you get a ⅜" galvanized bolt, also get ⅜" galvanized nuts and washers.

Nut

A nut is a threaded, hexagonal-shaped piece that screws onto a bolt. You use a wrench to secure the nut to the bolt, tightening it against the washer.

Washer

A washer is a flat, donut-shaped disc that slides over the bolt, before the washer goes on, creating a wide base for the nut to push against. Without the washer, the nut would dig into the wood, making it less stable.

CERAMIC MAGNET

These are magnets that are especially strong. Look for them at craft stores or hardware stores.

CONCRETE VS. CEMENT

Here is a secret that not many people know. Cement is an ingredient in concrete. It's like the flour to the cake batter. So now when you are walking down the sidewalk and someone says, "Don't trip on the cement!" you can be really annoying and say, "Well, actually, this is concrete. Cement is just one of the ingredients." You will lose friends, but your superior knowledge will make up for that.

Cement

Cement is more complicated than concrete, and it involves a lot of words like "calcination" and "chemically combine" that honestly I'm not qualified to explain. Basically, limestone goes through a crazy process and becomes cement. As with limestone, if you put your bare little hands or feet or arms or what-have-you in cement for long enough, you will get chemical burns—and they're terrible. My friend Allison did this in high school and got huge burns on her knees.

Cement All

Cement All is a combination of cement and sand. The reason we use it in the projects by Attalia and Khadija is because it's nice and smooth, and neither of those projects needed much in the way of structural support. Cement All is white, which means it dyes easily, and it looks good on its own.

Concrete

Concrete is basically cement plus rocks/sand/gravel plus water. You can make your own, but the best way to ensure a strong end result is to buy it premixed in a bag and add water.

Concrete Dye

I have found only two concrete dyes at large building-supply stores. One is a brown color and the other is terra-cotta—not that interesting, although Attalia used terra-cotta, and it turned out beautifully. We ordered some dyes online for Khadija's project, and they were okay but expensive. If you are determined to dye your concrete, you can go to a concrete supply store and do some investigating, or keep looking online.

DRYWALL ANCHOR

A drywall anchor (sometimes called a molly) is a mechanism used to help hang heavy objects in drywall. Here's why: These days, houses are built out of 2x lumber (2x4s, 2x6s, etc.), and the interior walls are covered with drywall, and drywall is not strong. There is a 16" to 24" gap between these pieces of wood, and sometimes the heavy thing you want to hang goes right between the wood. To help you hang that thing, you install an anchor into the drywall, creating a secure connection for you to screw. Some anchors require you to create a pilot hole, which you then screw the anchor into. Some anchors go into an even bigger hole, and as you run a screw through it, its little legs bend and grab the back of the drywall. It's pretty cool. There are many styles, so read the package to find the one that is best for your project.

FASTENER

You have two main types of fasteners: nails and screws. Within those two categories there are about a bazillion different types. It's important to know specifically what type of fastener you need, so read your directions well. I hope that as you learn, you'll be able to anticipate which type of fasteners to use before you are told. It's going to be great. Here is one important trick to anticipating the length of fastener you need: You want more than half of the fastener to be in your second piece of wood once the fastener is completely driven in. For example, if you are attaching a 1½"-thick board to another board, you want a screw or nail that is over 3". Why? The first 1½" goes into the first board, and you want more than that to go into the second board. If your second board is thinner than your first, see if you can simply run the screw in the opposite direction so it goes through the thinner board first. In this scenario, it's not secure to run the screw through the thick board first. I have to tell you, this can be complicated, but put this fact in your pocket and use it when it makes sense.

Nail Coatings

Bright

A bright nail means there is no coating. These types of nails can be used on small projects, like Soleil's Magnet Board, or to hang a picture in your house. They should only be used for inside projects.

Galvanized

A galvanized nail is coated in zinc, which looks like a chunky gray material. These nails won't rust easily and are for exterior use. They should also be used if you are nailing into pressure-treated wood. The chemicals in this wood will eat away at a nongalvanized nail. Galvanized nails have a purpose, but they also bend really easily. In order to keep your frustration level low, only use them when necessary.

Vinyl-Coated Sinkers

These nails are most commonly used when framing houses. There are two cool things about them. First, they are coated in a slick, oily substance that helps the nails slide in easily. Why? When you are building something big like a house (or shed or playhouse), you are driving in *a lot* of nails. You want this task to be as easy as possible, and that slick coating helps. The other cool thing? These nails have a grippy head that looks like a waffle. When the head of the hammer meets the head of the nail, they become best friends, joining easily and happily each time the hammer strikes the nail. (In real life, your best friend should never hit you. That's my public service announcement for the day.) Anyway, it's pretty cool the way these nails help you work a little more easily.

Nail Types

Brad

Brads are itty-bitty nails with just the slightest little head. You can use them inside or outside (get galvanized!) for finish work. Reba's Salvaged Shelf could use brads to secure the boards together (although Reba used screws). The small head on a brad nail allows you to sink the nail with a nail set and then fill the hole with wood putty. Sand it down and stain it, and people will forever wonder where that nail went!

Duplex

You will likely never use this nail, but again, it's fun to know about. It is essentially a nail with two heads. (Two heads! I know!) The heads are stacked about ¼" apart. The whole point of these nails, unlike ring shanks and spiral shanks (see below), is to be able to take them out. They are used primarily in concrete forms. The first head (the one that is lower on the shaft) holds the form (a piece of plywood) in place. Once the concrete is poured and dried between the vertical pieces of plywood, the second head allows someone to slide a hammer behind it and pull the nail out. Amazing! Why do they need to come out so easily? Concrete forms are built to come apart after a concrete pour, and if the nails come out more easily, the work is done quicker—saving big bucks and a lot of frustration.

Finish nail

I could basically copy everything I said about brad nails and paste it here, so go reread that section and come back. The main difference between brads and finish nails is that finish nails are a little thicker, making them stronger. The heads on finish nails are a little bigger. That's it. For every project in this book, honestly, use whatever you accidentally bought at the store. It's fine.

Ring shank

Ring shank nails are the most fun. You will likely never use them though. A ring shank nail has little metal donuts that run up the shaft of the nail. Their purpose is to hold the nail in place. It seems like you'd want this on every nail, right? Not really. These nails are most commonly used for flooring, and the little donuts keep the nails from sliding out of the flooring. When regular nails are used, they can eventually slide out of flooring, making that squeaking noise you hear when you are walking on older wooden floors (or poorly installed new floors). Now you know!

Roofing nail

Roofing nails are short, fat nails with a wide head, and they invite your hammer to smash your finger. Here is a trick I learned—if you are using roofing nails, turn your fingers over so the pads are facing up while you hold the nail instead of your fingernails facing up. The pads of your fingers are a lot more forgiving than your fingernails. Good luck!

Spiral shank

Spiral shank nails are really cool, but I don't think I have ever used one. Like ring shanks, they are used for flooring, the idea being that the spiral will keep the nail from sliding out.

Nails

Nails have a variety of purposes, from connecting the wood that makes houses to being hidden in the joints of furniture. There are many types of nails, and we will go over several of them here. The biggest distinction between a nail and a screw? You hit a nail with a hammer instead of driving it in with a drill, impact driver, or screwdriver. (Screws are threaded, and nails are not.)

When you are looking at nails, you will see the letter "d" a lot. What does the "d" stand for? Here's another pro tip: Don't say this letter. Every time you see it, say the word "penny." Let's practice: "8d galvanized nail" is "eight penny galvanized nail." Good job! The numbers stand for size. The lower the number, the shorter and thinner the nail. The higher the number, the longer and thicker the nail. An 8d nail is 1½" long, which is pretty average. A 16d nail is about the biggest you'll ever use, and a 4d nail is about the smallest. Oh, and in the unlikely chance you are building a house with a framing crew, you can just use the number to talk about these nails—eights, sixteens, etc. Everyone will be so impressed.

Screws

What's the difference between a screw and a nail? Well, a lot. First, let's talk about what tools you use with a screw. In order to drive a screw into a piece of wood or metal or anything, you need a drill, impact driver, or a screwdriver. You can't just pound it in—you have to turn it. Screws are very, very useful. One thing to know about screws, though, is that they don't have a lot of sheer resistance. What does that mean? Let's say you want to build a really tall shelf outside—like, 10' tall and 10' long. You use 2x4s and screws, and you do a great job and it's beautiful (and easier to put together than if you'd used nails). One day, a big rock falls from the sky. It's heavy but isn't a meteor. This rock lands right on your shelf. You know what the screws do? *They break off.* Now, in a parallel universe, you build that huge shelf with nails. When the rock falls, what do the nails do? They bend. But screws are great. Use them. Also, in the falling-rock scenario, your beautiful shelf is still pretty darn broken, no matter which fastener you used.

Exterior screws

Exterior screws have a special coating on them so they don't rust, bleed, rot, and break. Here is a secret for you, though. I really like exterior screws because of that coating, and I use them *inside* the house too. I know. It's wild. That coating helps the screws go in very easily, kind of like the vinyl coating we talked about in the nails section.

Here are a few common screws (both interior and exterior):

- 3″ exterior screws: These are exterior screws that are 3″ long.
- 1½″ interior or exterior screws: These are screws that can be used only inside (interior screws) or inside and outside (exterior screws) and are 1½″ long.
- 1½″ wood screws: These screws are 1½″ long and have a coarse thread.
- ¾″ screws with a flat, countersunk head: These are itty-bitty screws, only ¾″ long. Countersunk screws have a flat top, and under that flat top the screw head is angled, like a funnel.

Interior screws

Interior screws are not weather resistant, so if you used them outside they would do a few annoying things: rust, bleed rust on the nice thing you built, rot, and break. Does that persuade you to use exterior screws? It should. Use interior screws only on projects that will stay indoors.

Screw head types

There are many types of screw heads, and it's important to understand the differences so you can select the right bit *and* pick the screw that works best for you. The various types of screw heads are covered in detail in the chapter on tools at the beginning of this book. You can review that section any time you want a refresher course on screw heads. The big takeaway is to be familiar with the names and shapes of the common types of screw heads:

- Flathead (aka slotted)
- Phillips
- Star drive (aka Torx)
- Square drive

There are a few other types, but they are less common. The most important thing is to make sure you have a bit to match.

Screw threading

Screws generally have one of two types of thread: coarse or fine. These are just what you would expect. Coarse threads are wider apart, and fine threads are tighter together. Most screws are coarse threaded, but some are fine threaded, like drywall screws.

HARDWOOD

Hardwood refers to the type of tree the wood comes from. The wood of some trees is denser (harder) than that of others. Walnut, cherry, maple, oak, and mahogany are common hardwoods. If you go to a woodworking store with a parent/chaperone, you can wander around and look at all the many types of beautiful woods. There is a wood called purple heart, and you should get your eyes on it at least once in your life.

PALLET

Pallets are wooden platforms that are used to deliver large items. They can often be found behind stores, next to dumpsters, or at your local hardware store (just ask). Chances are your neighbors might even have one lying around. Ask your friends!

ROPE

Rope can be made of many different materials and comes in many different styles. It can be single-braided, double-braided, diamond-braided, hollow, twisted, plaited, or more. It can be made of natural fibers or synthetic fibers. We don't need to get into all of that here, but you are welcome to dive into types of rope on your own. It *is* interesting. Samantha's swing project encourages you to choose the color and style you'd like—so you can select synthetic or natural, blue or brown or rainbow, as long as it is ½" in diameter.

SAND

You can buy sand from most hardware stores, small or big. If you are making Attalia's project, you could use any sort of container—a cardboard box, a shallow plastic bin—and fill it with sand. If the sand is a little wet, it will actually help the holes hold their shapes.

SANDPAPER

Sandpaper is a gritty paper that, when rubbed over wood or another surface, smooths it out. The lower the grit, the rougher the sandpaper. Likewise, the higher the grit, the smoother the sandpaper. When sanding, start with a lower grit and then move on to a higher grit. For example, if you were doing a simple wood project and using pretty rough wood, you might start with an 80-grit, then 120, then 200. Be careful! If the wood is already kind of smooth, start at 120 or 150. Otherwise, a lower-grit sandpaper will make the wood rougher, which is not what you want.

- 80-grit sandpaper: This is rougher sandpaper that can be used when starting out sanding a project.
- 150-grit sandpaper: This is a medium-grit sandpaper. Use it if your wood is already quite smooth, or after you've sanded your project with 80- or 100-grit sandpaper.
- 220-grit sandpaper: This sandpaper is the most common high-grit sandpaper, and can be found in most hardware or lumber stores.

TRIANGLE RING HANGER WITH NAILS OR SCREWS

A picture is worth a thousand words.

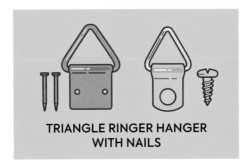

TRIANGLE RINGER HANGER WITH NAILS

WIRE

Wire comes in different gauges. Higher-gauge wire is thinner, and lower-gauge wire is thicker. Crazy, I know. If you want the wire to hold its form while you shape it (for example, in Tanzira's Tea Light Luminaries), go for 16- or 20-gauge wire.

WOOD

Dimensions of Wood

The first thing to know is that many woods are usually referred to in dimensions—for example, 2x4, 4x4, 2x6, etc. The first number is the thickness of the board (in inches) and the second number is the width (also in inches). This is called dimensional lumber. Sometimes there is a third number tacked onto the end, like 2x4x8. This is slightly confusing because the first two numbers are inches, and the third is feet. So a 2x4x8 is a 2x4 that is 8' long.

When you see that "x" between the numbers, you say "by." You may have already known this, but now you know for sure. Here's the other thing you should know: Builders often refer to lumber by the first number and then that x. For example, if I was on a jobsite and there was a huge stack of 2x4s, I would say, "I'm going to grab some two-bys." That's it. Or sometimes you just need something for its thickness,

and you don't care how wide it is. You can say, "I need a four-foot one-by." This is generally used when you're referring to scrap rather than something you would say in a lumber store.

Here is some information that will change your world. Ready to learn the truth about those numbers?

- 2x4: A 2x4 is actually only 1½" x 3½". Generally speaking, you take half an inch off whatever the measurement says. There are some exceptions (keep reading).
- 1x: Anything that starts with "1x" is actually ¾" thick.
- x8, x10, x12: These measurements are missing ¾", so, for example, a 1x8 is actually ¾" x 7¼". It's tough. I know.
- ⁵⁄₄: Here's a fun one. This is pronounced "five quarter," and it essentially means, "Fine, you're stealing a quarter inch off my wood? I'll order an extra then." So, ⁵⁄₄" wood is actually 1". You may never need to order this size wood, but I hope someday you can stroll into a lumberyard and order it like a boss.

Here's how to order wood. Remember that 2x4x8 means 2" x 4" x 8'. Again, the first two numbers are in inches, and the last is in feet. If you walk into a lumber store and want four 8' long 2x4s, you simply say, "I need four 2x4x8s."

Here are some dimensions of wood that you'll see in projects in this book:

- 2x4: This simply means any 2x4 that is not made of special wood, like cedar. It is usually pine or Douglas fir.
- 1x4: A 1x4 is ¾" thick and 3½" wide, and can be any material.
- 1x6: A 1x6 is ¾" thick x 5½" wide and can be any material.
- 4x4: Any guesses on this one? It's 3½" thick and 3½" wide. You're really getting the hang of this. And it can be made out of any material.
- 1x6x8 cedar: ¾" x 5½" x 7¼'. I know. And in this case, the material is cedar. The big question: tight knot or clear? That's up to you—tight knot is the cheaper option (see the next page for more about cedar).
- 4x4x8, not cedar or juniper: This is for Aleeyah's Mason Bee House. Why can't it be made of the really great, weather-resistant, bug-resistant cedar or juniper, which are both excellent to use outdoors? This is a good thought until you remember that . . . bees are bugs! Yes, they are, and we really don't want to kill them, which is why you are making them a house. So go get yourself some nice 4x4 Doug fir or pine. The bees thank you.
- 2x10 or 2x12, about 6' long: This is for Alice's Chicken Ladder. You might not have wood lying around like they do on a farm, so go to the lumber store and look at the wood. Decide if you want a wider

ramp (2x12) or a narrower one (2x10). Then decide how much you love your chickens. Are you going to splurge on cedar? Truth be told, we didn't. Chickens are a hot mess, and they poop on everything. So we went cheap on this one.

- 8' 2x2 cedar boards: Remember, 2x2 cedar is really 1½" x 1½".

- 1 piece of ¾" plywood, measuring 2' x 2': Please note that this says 2' (two feet) not 2" (two inches). As mentioned in Brooke's Jigsaw Puzzle, many of the popular DIY lumber stores carry ¾" plywood precut to 2'x2', which will make your life a little easier.

- Lath: Lath is a material commonly found in old homes under the plaster on the walls. Some cities and towns have a salvaged building supply store. If so, they surely have lath that they would be really happy to sell to you for cheap. If you don't have such a store nearby, you can still buy lath new. It's just not as fun.

Types of Wood

This section covers a few types of wood, but it's not a complete list of every type.

Exterior-use wood

If you are building a project that will stay outside with no cover, like a garden box or little library, you need wood that won't easily rot. There are three common types of wood used for outdoors: cedar, juniper, and pressure-treated.

CEDAR: Cedar is the most common nontreated lumber. It's a little more expensive, but many people like the look, and the fact that it doesn't have added chemicals. It is a soft wood, so you don't want to use it for something structural, like building a house, where the wood has to support a lot of weight. But for most outdoor projects, cedar is great. There are different grades of cedar:

- Tight knot: Tight knot cedar is the cheaper option. This term means that you can easily see the knots. Most people don't mind, and for many projects, tight knot cedar is the easy choice.

- Clear: Clear cedar means there are no knots visible to the naked eye. The grain of the wood runs beautifully uninterrupted throughout the entire piece. Clear cedar costs about twice as much as tight knot cedar.

JUNIPER: Western juniper is a newer product and is not available everywhere. Juniper is considered an almost-invasive species, making it a good product to harvest. Juniper is very rot resistant and is ideal for fence posts and garden beds. Have extra bits ready, as this wood puts up a bit of a fight, so you may end up breaking a few bits.

PRESSURE-TREATED: Pressure-treated wood is a common wood, like Doug fir, that has been injected with chemicals to make it able to withstand exterior weather. *Never use this wood for garden beds, as the chemicals can leach into the soil, or for children's play structures, including swings.* You do not want tiny hands touching it daily. You can use pressure-treated wood for fence posts and other structural applications, like foundations.

Plywood

Even though plywood is a type of sheet good, it's so important and it's used so often that I'm giving it its very own section.

All the other types of sheet goods are, in one way or another, small pieces of wood glued together. Plywood is different. Plywood is made up of large, very thin sheets of wood glued together in layers. Plywood runs from very affordable (a little more expensive than OSB) to very expensive. You can use plywood under your floor where no one will see it, or you can build beautiful cabinets out of it.

There are many grades of plywood, and learning them all can be confusing. But before you get intimidated, you need to know something. It's really fun to walk into the lumber store and say, "I need four pieces of ¾" 4x8 CCX." But you know what I also do *a lot*? I walk in, tired, and I say, "I don't have all the words, and I need you to tell me what I need. I want some cheap ¾" plywood, because no one is ever going to see it." They laugh, ask me what I'm building, and we go from there. Now, to contradict myself, I am a *big* advocate of using the correct terminology. I make eight-year-olds learn the difference between 8d and 16d nails, for Pete's sake, but you don't have to learn and memorize every grade of plywood. However, if you want to, here you go.

THE LETTERS: With plywood, the first letter you say means the front, and the second letter means the back. So, for example, my sister decided to put plywood floors down in her kitchen and just seal the heck out of it (fingers crossed). We used ACX—the front was nice (A), the back was not (C), and it could withstand a little moisture (X). Here's what those letters mean:

- A: This is the nice stuff. And expensive. If you are building cabinets, you are going to want AA—nice on the front and back. But for other applications, you might be able to get away with using A on one side only, which is a little cheaper.

- B: This is still nice, but it has some manufacturer-made repairs. For example, if there is a little hole from a loose knot, they will fill it with wood filler and sand it down.

- C: This is, in my mind, the typical grade used for common projects. For all my house-framing work, we always ordered CDX—mildly decent on one side, kind of terrible on the other, mildly weather resistant. Technically the difference between C and D is the size of the holes and the cracks. For C grade, the holes will not be larger than 1½″ (and will be filled by the manufacturer).

- D: You'll have some holes up to 2½″ in diameter. For some projects, this is totally fine because, again, it will be filled by the manufacturer.

TYPES: Besides the grade, you might want to learn about the different types of plywood.

- Regular ol' plywood: This is the stuff you are directed to when you walk into a large home center and say, "I need some plywood." It's basic, and it comes in a few thicknesses and a few grades.
- Hardwood plywood: This is a nice product that has been covered with a sheet of hardwood. It looks fancy, and you can make projects like furniture or cabinets out of it.
- Baltic birch or ApplePly: This plywood is pretty nice and is often used for modern furniture. Birch has a softer finish, whereas ApplePly has a nice hardwood finish.

Sheet goods

Sheet goods are manufactured wood products that generally come in 4′ by 8′ sheets (you can get them in various lengths and widths, but this is the most common size). There are many kinds. They come in various thicknesses, from ⅛″ to 1¼″.

MDF: MDF stands for "medium-density fiberboard." MDF is like really, really dense particle board. It's made of cellulose (fibers that come from trees and other plants) and resin (a sticky substance that also comes from trees and other plants). It has some good uses, because it is thicker, but it is not a good substitute for real wood. Sometimes trim inside a house is made of MDF, or you can use it for things like closet shelves (which are often made of melanine). Confused yet? Just remember that MDF is very heavy, and you can't see the bits (or particles) as easily as you can with particle board.

MELAMINE: Melamine is particle board covered with a thin layer of plastic. It is often used to make cabinets and the like. As with particle board, though, it basically melts when it gets wet, and it breaks easily.

OSB: OSB stands for "oriented strand board." OSB is great for projects that will not remain outside, like the inside layer of a playhouse roof. Some people even get creative and use it on floors, liking the textured look. This product is cheaper than plywood, but is less durable. It's perfectly fine for rough projects that will remain dry, but you would never want to use it for a finished project or something outside. That being said, OSB is a sound structural product.

PARTICLE BOARD: People often mix up particle board and OSB. Particle board is made of tiny, tiny bits of wood, almost sawdust, mixed with glue, then laid out flat and compressed into thick sheets. Particle board is not structural, and is generally used on top of another sheet good. For example, when laying a floor, you might put particle board on top of OSB; then you would lay flooring on top of the particle board. Particle board breaks easily, and is ruined when it gets wet (remember, it's made from glue and sawdust). Some furniture is made of particle board, which is why it breaks so easily.

WOOD FINISH

Wood finishes are used to dress up and protect wood. Many woodworkers have a favorite finish, and sometimes they cover that finish with wax. I am not a professional woodworker, so for my hobby habit, I use a water-based finish, like polyurethane (commonly called "poly"). Why use water-based? It's easier to clean up. That's all. If you love research, get out your books or your internet, and dive deep into the world of oil-based versus water-based finishes. But if you've built a cool little project and you want to do the easy thing, buy yourself some water-based polyurethane. When you're done applying the finish, clean your rags and hands with soap and water. If you choose to buy an oil-based poly, you will need paint thinner or mineral spirits to clean it up. And if it's an exterior project? You are stuck with oil-based, my friend.

One big note: When applying any sort of finish you need to (a) be in a well-ventilated area, and (b) be re-e-ally careful with cleanup, and follow every direction. Some finishes, like linseed oil and Danish oils, are spontaneously combustible. What does this mean? It means that you are excited to put the finish on your project, so you use a clean rag to gently, lovingly apply the finish. Then you leave the rag on the table or in a trash can or on your fence, like my parents did, and *the rag catches itself on fire! By itself. Just up and catches itself on fire!* So don't play with that. Read the directions and put it away properly. One thing you can do to be prepared is this: While you are buying the finish, ask if the hardware store sells an empty metal paint can with a lid. Take it home, and when you are finishing applying the finish on your new project, you can lock your rag up in that empty, brand-new paint can, and your night will be a lot better. Oh, another less important note: You will want to apply more than one coat of finish on your project. Like three coats. Or four.

WOOD WAX

Wood wax is really great and fun to use. I am talking specifically about liquid wax (there is also paste wax). Use a rag to apply the liquid wax after your finish has dried. Let your wax dry, and then rub it down with a dry rag to make it shine.

ACKNOWLEDGMENTS

This book is definitely the effort, input, and support of so many people. I'm often stunned when I recount all the people who believed in and supported me.

The staff at University of Portland and Bon Appetit who supported me from day one (looking at you, too, Bill Reed) and continue to support me and the work unconditionally. Jessica Murphy Moo, for supporting me with the introduction and helping me come full circle, writing the piece I never could for Brian. I am indebted.

Ev, thank you for stepping up when I needed to sit down and type. You took on so much of Girls Build this last year and made it even greater. Without you I couldn't have completed this book without losing my mind or Girls Build. Bubble tea date soon?

The Girls Build team is the best team I've ever been on. You work the hardest and laugh the best. You keep me on my toes and keep a smile on my face. You are dedicated to the mission and to the campers, passing on skills but also simply teaching the very best way to navigate life. Thank you for bringing yourselves to the table and giving Girls Build your all.

The Girls Build board, who believe in Girls Build and me, who always have my back while continuing to propel us forward. You #ellenvate me.

Connie Ashbrook, for being a trailblazer, and, as you once put it, "stepping out of my way" when you believed in what I was doing. Thank you for giving me the blessing and courage to start Girls Build.

Dawn Jones Redstone, oh man, there is so much to say. Thanks for the headphones way back when, for always challenging me even when I get annoyed, for always believing in what I do and think, for making me laugh every day for, like, 10 years and for just being with me every step of the way.

Ashley, I know this book made your life so hard, but thanks for stepping up anyway and pestering me when necessary. You made room for me to do my job and write this book, while letting me vent and helping me laugh. You made Girls Build run so smoothly so that I could actually have the time to write. I'm glad we're on this journey together!

Joleen, you're the very best "volunteer" I could ask for. Thank you for always being down to troubleshoot, to eat good food, for hot tub meetings, and for bringing Girls Build to the next level. You're fantastic.

Jenny Lewis, look at that! Thanks for believing in me and this book and for letting me cry sometimes.

All the photographers: Each of you showed off a different style and captured the girls so well. I kept finding myself amazed and excited as you flipped your cameras to me to show off the cool photo you'd just taken. Thank you for making this book so special.

To some guy named Mike (Rowe), you took a chance on me and I can't thank you enough. Your support has kept me motivated and has lifted up our mission in ways I could never have anticipated. Thanks for your belief in the joy and life-changing ability of working with one's hands.

Elaine at Girls Who Work, Judaline at Tools and Tiaras, Cia at Electric Girls, Whitney and Renee at The Twine Lab, John at The MiLL, Sonia and Chrissy at Northwest Maritime Center—thank you for opening your doors and collaborating to shine a light on your girls. Thank you for supporting girls in the trades every day in all you do. You put your hearts into this work, furthering the mission and helping change the future of the trades. Thank you for your selflessness and your passion.

Emily from Girls Garage, you've been an advocate from the start. Thanks for always being there to say something encouraging, answer questions, and basically just say, "We'll make it through!" It's been incredible to have your support and to watch Girls Garage grow. Well done.

Sara Richardson—thank you for finding our Cabo girls, for all your work leading up to the trip: then, during, and after. Sorry for your incredible sunburn, but thank you for dragging me through Cabo in the heat during a very busy life and capturing the essence of these girls so well.

Abbot, Cat, Abra, Sommer, Cara, Becca—WE ARE NOT BANGING PIPES ON THE FLOOR. Thank you for making a work week relaxing and putting up with me assembling stools and tables in our room all week long, for taking a group date to Home Depot, and for making me laugh always and forever. May we all someday open Som Som's Boogie Push.

To the La Taq staff, thanks for letting me sit in the corner with headphones on, drinking margaritas and eating various cheese items without asking questions or worrying that I was taking up too much space. I wrote much of this while sitting at your tables while my children were blocks away, not bothering me. Much appreciated.

Leigh, thanks for taking so much time to meet with me and write up the plans for the sheet metal projects, even though they didn't end up in the book. The book wouldn't have been completed without your critical help. Thank you for wanting to pass your motivation and passion on to the next generation.

Rebecca Beamer, thank you for helping get this proposal out the door! Your drawings were so important, and I am forever grateful that you were willing to whip something up (my words, not yours—I think it was harder than that). And, of course, for facilitating making the world a wider place for Girls Build girls.

Heather Binns, what would this book be without your photographs? You took a chance and a big leap to help make this project a reality, and without your skills (you too, Bill!) and belief in the mission, this book wouldn't have happened. Not only your actual photography skills, but your help in finding the right girls and locations (hello to the Croft Farm! Thank you too!) and taking the first photos on a promise and some hope. I'm so glad you were a big part of this.

To all the folks who tested these projects: Mom (forever my champion); Lindsay; Leah; Drew (and Carlos, Alex, Spencer, and Andrew); Molly and Gavin, who worked in the freezing cold; Sue and Lucy; Sarah and Megan; Sammmmm! and Amanda; Jeannie and Rebekah (so incredibly meticulous); April (you had the most uplifting notes!); Kadja; Asa; Ea; Io; Tuulie; Justin; Corina; Rachel; Annaliese; and Jenneke. Thank you for being a critical part of this process, finding bumps, digging in, and ultimately making these projects a possible and reliable part of the book.

Lisa and the whole team at Black Dog, you were excited about this book before the proposal was even started! Thank you for being so engaging and ready, for teaching me how to navigate this world, and for simply being a group of women ready and willing to support this project and its mission.

Jan, I laugh when I think that I started this all without you. It would have been a hot, hot mess. I appreciate you in all the ways and am so grateful for your frank and honest support and your incredible eye in all things photography.

Ilana Gurevich, for pushing me always in a forward direction and helping me see my own worth and value.

Jenny! Remember that time you called me out of the blue and asked if I wanted to write a book? Thanks for letting me call you and leave messages without identifying myself, rolling your eyes (I can hear it over the phone) when I say, "Who dis?" too often and for generally encouraging and motivating me at every turn. I can't wait to teach Carmen to build you those bookshelves.

hhh, thanks for sticking with me all these years, for supporting this book, being my sounding board and bringing levity to everything. I can always count on you.

Sue Ledgerwood, for taking this seriously from the start and being my "novice eyes" on the plans. I couldn't have made it work without your meticulous eye. Also, just thanks for always being the best.

Catpcheng. What would I be without you? You are the person who gets all my jokes, lets me cry so hard, and trades incredible graphic design work for fence building. This book wouldn't exist if it wasn't for your belief in me and willingness to give me your all. Thank you for all the La Taq dates, for still hanging out with me even though I have kids now, and for just always doing the right and best thing. Boop! (Hi, Fan and Yao!)

Maria, you pave the way every day for the next generation, and I know it's not easy. You got out there, strapped on some boots, and picked up some tools when your life was at its lowest. You have worked so hard for what you have today, and I am so proud of you.

Bridget, thank you for having a basement that is kidproof, an always-open bottle of wine, and a magical massage machine, all of which kept me sane and capable of moving forward. Thank you for being real with me and, from the start, being my champion.

Daddy—I wish you could have been here for all of this, but I know you see it all. I like to think you passed so much on to me, and I am proud of that. Thank you for your wit and humor, your curly hair, your penchant for "borrowing," and for inspiring us all to be good and giving people.

David, I never imagined that my mom could be so happy and so well loved. Thank you for being a father to us, for bringing my mom joy, for loving my boys and just being an all-around good man. And, of course, for being so excited about this book.

Oh, Mom. Thank you for calling me nearly every day to tell me that Barack Obama had to give back his advance and that I better keep writing. You really pushed me, doing the math—again, nearly every day—on how many projects I would have to complete per week if I wanted to finish on time. For watching my kids so I could write in coffee shops, even though my kids are bonkers. For being the first strong woman I knew, who made do with what we had, teaching me that you can't break what's already broken, so you might as well take it apart. Thanks for instilling curiosity in all three of us and letting me and Bridget do and build whatever we wanted. Thank you for fighting for us when things got rough, for showing that you always, always have my back. You are my very favorite mom.

My boys, who did their best at every turn to thwart my efforts. You're cute and funny and crazy making, but you also think that every tool is "for Girls Build" and that every construction worker is a woman. You showed me that representing women and girls working and learning construction can truly change the way that little minds think. Plus, you made sure I laughed every day. I love you so much.

Kendal, this was not your favorite year, but this book wouldn't exist without your support. Thank you for the solo Saturday mornings you granted me, the push to take a weekend away from everyone and everything to simply get it done, and for supporting Girls Build from the start. You believed in me and the mission thoroughly, and although it all makes you crazy, you show up every time, in whatever way is needed. I can't thank you enough.

To all the parents of the incredible souls featured in this book: Good on you for elevating your daughters, for believing in them and supporting them as they explore the world in a way that makes sense to them. You are helping the future, and it looks pretty bright.

Finally, the girls. You are strong, courageous, and bold. Your strength shows through in all that you do. You fight battles every day—to be seen, to be heard, to get through rough days with your heads held high, to be your best selves in a world that is fighting you. I believe in you, am proud of you, and draw inspiration from you daily. Go forth and be the world.

IMAGE CREDITS

Special thanks to the photographers who contributed to this book.

Ashley Crenshaw: 84, 86

Heather Binns: 12, 19, 43, 48–49, 60, 62, 80, 83, 92, 130, 148, 152, 154, 176, 178, 180, 182, 190, 193, 194, 197, 198, 210, 212, 230, 239, 241

Kelsey Brunner: 94, 97, 106, 108, 118, 188, 204, 207, 224, 227, 228

Whitney Fox: 4, 78, 120, 128, 138, 140, 162, 222

Chris Ho/Chris Ho Photography: viii, xi

Emily Kask: xiv, 66, 164, 167

Katharine Kimball: 208

Massabesic Audubon Center, 120

Sara Richardson: 122, 124, 168, 170, 220

Anna Solo: 50, 68, 70, 98, 101, 102, 110, 113, 114, 132

Jan Sonnenmair: 52, 55, 56, 58, 72, 74, 142, 144, 150, 242, 244

INDEX

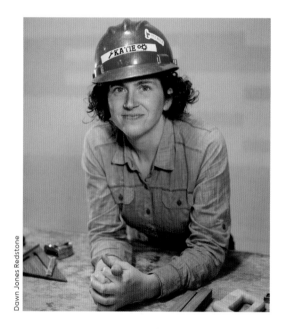

Dawn Jones Redstone

ABOUT THE AUTHOR

KATIE HUGHES is the founder of Girls Build, an organization created in 2016. Based in Portland, Oregon, Girls Build offers girls ages 8 to 14 the chance to learn mechanical and electrical skills as well as wood- and metalworking.

girlsbuild.org   🐦 girlsbuildpdx   🅵 girlsbuild